THREE NUNS *from the* RANCH

Sister Kathleen Cogan

Benet Hill Monastery

All Rights Reserved

Published by Benet Hill Monastery of Colorado Springs, Inc.

3190 Benet Lane

Colorado Springs, Colorado 80921

Editor: Karen Brock

Design: Liz Mrofka, lizmrofka.com

Printed by: CreateSpace

ISBN-13: 978-1975807498
ISBN-10: 1975807499

ACKNOWLEDGEMENTS

This book could never have been written without the help of Sister Leann and Sister Elizabeth who each contributed her own memories.

This book could never have been finished without the kindness and expertise of Karen Brock who edited the final copy and Liz Mrofka who designed and produced the book.

Special thanks to Aimee and Jim Farrell who introduced us to Karen Brock, the editor of this book.

INTRODUCTION

In late 2013, it became necessary for me to retire from internal ministry in the monastery finance office. Because of peripheral neuropathy, I was having difficulty keeping my balance even while using a walker, and I had fallen several times. In December of that year I received an infusion of new medication. In other patients, this medicine had successfully slowed or stopped the deterioration of their peripheral nerves. However, after four infusions, I became critically ill from an allergic reaction to the medicine. I was hospitalized for two weeks, at first not recognizing even my sisters Leann and Elizabeth. After the hospital, I was in a rehabilitation center for a month. Sometime during the total six weeks of medical care, I had a slight left-sided stroke. With the help of a therapist, I relearned how to walk but still needed to use a walker. When I returned to Benet Hill, I began falling more frequently until in July of 2014, I became a permanent wheelchair patient.

Recently, I have become realistically aware of what Jesus said to Peter: "Amen, amen, I say to you, when you were younger, you used to dress yourself and go where you wanted; but when you grow old, you will stretch out your hands, and somebody else will dress you and lead you where you do not want to go" (John 21: 18). I now need help with some of my personal chores. Whenever I get out of my wheelchair, wishing to walk with my walker, a nurse or an aide needs to stabilize me, holding fast to a gait belt around my waist, as she walks with me. I am very aware that Jesus concluded his words to Peter by saying, "Follow me."

To do something that might help me regain more mental acuity, I decided at least to try writing a story, which has turned into a book about the three of us sisters from the ranch. This feat has been a slow, challenging, but valuable process. Because my memory has also been affected, it has been necessary for me to rely on other family members to help me remember some past and recent facts for this book. Working on the book has helped me to keep occupied, busy, and happy, as well as to remain interested in life.

Throughout this book you will read "Mount Saint Scholastica Convent in Atchison, Kansas," or just "The Mount." At other times you will read "Benet Hill Monastery" or just "Benet Hill." All three of us entered the convent at Mount Saint Scholastica. Later, we became charter members of Benet Hill as I explain next. With growing numbers in the membership of Mount St. Scholastica Convent in Atchison, Kansas, the decision was made to start a new community, which we call a "daughter-house." The Mount already had started one in Mexico City, Mexico, and one in Glendora, California. Because The Mount already had many Colorado missions, it was decided to start this new house in Colorado, to serve the existing missions there. When suitable property was listed for sale in Colorado Springs, The Mount purchased it as the site for Benet Hill Priory, as the new daughter-house was to be named. Each member of The Mount was given a choice of one of three options: I want to go to Colorado; I prefer not to go to Colorado, but will go if I am sent; I do not want to go to Colorado. Could you possibly guess which option we three chose? Benet Hill Priory was a dependent daughter-house for three years, to insure its viability. At the end of three years, we again had to choose whether to return to the Mount or to permanently transfer our vows to Benet Hill Priory. In 1965, we transferred our vows and became charter members of Benet Hill Priory. In later years, we reclaimed the original name of Benedictine women's and men's communities and became Benet Hill Monastery. The writing of this book was begun in 2015 during the year-long celebration of Benet Hill's fiftieth anniversary. Our new monastery on Chelton Road was within one hundred miles of the Cogan Ranch. In our new Mother House, each sister had, for the very first time, a yearly two-week vacation. Those changes made possible many of the occurrences mentioned in this book. Individual memories throughout the book are not necessarily in chronological order.

TABLE OF CONTENTS

♣

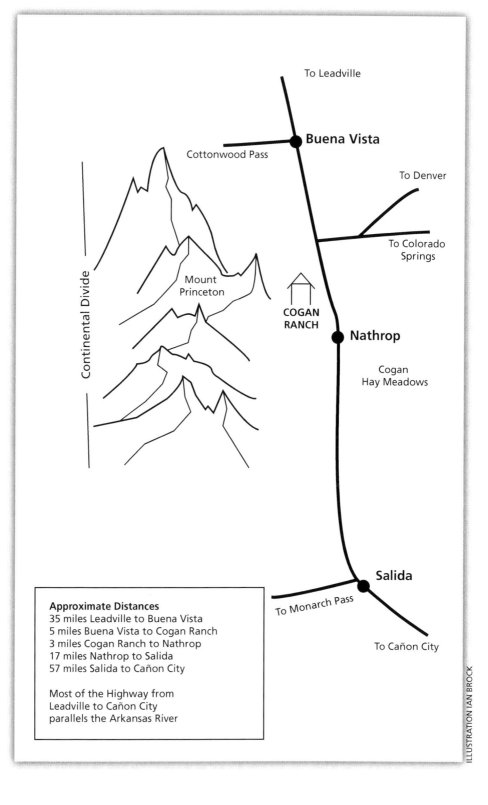

To Leadville

Buena Vista

Cottonwood Pass

To Denver

To Colorado Springs

Mount Princeton

Continental Divide

COGAN RANCH

Nathrop

Cogan Hay Meadows

Salida

To Monarch Pass

To Cañon City

Approximate Distances
35 miles Leadville to Buena Vista
5 miles Buena Vista to Cogan Ranch
3 miles Cogan Ranch to Nathrop
17 miles Nathrop to Salida
57 miles Salida to Cañon City

Most of the Highway from
Leadville to Cañon City
parallels the Arkansas River

ILLUSTRATION IAN BROCK

CHAPTER I
The Cogan Family

This book about three nuns would never be complete without a short family background explaining how we were gifted to grow up with wonderful parents on a special homestead ranch, which even today, is owned by a family member.

Jeremiah Cogan, our paternal grandfather from Ireland, was falsely accused of being a rebel leader of the Irish Resistance, at which time the Irish males were commonly called "The White Boys." Because of the accusation, Jeremiah was forced with a price on his head to flee his native home in the late 1870s, leaving his wife and their five children in County Cork, Ireland. He came to the United States and got a job working on the railroad at Nathrop, Colorado. Strange, but true, Nathrop, Colorado, where he initially came to find a job, is about three miles away from our first and current home ranch.

In 1883, Grandpa Jeremiah's wife Anne, and their five children came from Ireland to New York City where Grandpa met them and brought them to Nathrop. Our father John had been born June 1, 1878 in Ireland.

At last the family members were together. Shortly after their arrival, they left Nathrop and went to Fremont Pass, Colorado, where Grandpa was the railroad station agent. That winter they were totally snow bound for eighty-two days without anyone being able to reach them even by horse or sleigh. That time has been called, "The historic winter of '83." For entertainment, their youngest son John (Jack), our Dad, learned to ski on barrel staves. After that ordeal, they moved to Frisco, Colorado, for two years, but because of the snow and cold they moved back to Nathrop, where Grandpa then worked for the Rio Grande Railroad as a section hand. His wife Anne, our Grandmother, cooked for and served food to the section workers. One day, Grandpa Jeremiah found a calf on the railroad with a broken leg. Instead of killing it, as the other workers advised, he took it home, splinted the leg, and gave the calf into the care of his two youngest sons, Dad and his older brother William (Uncle Bill.) They cared for their new charge and the leg healed well. The calf prospered, and became everyone's pet. Soon the calf got into trouble because he did "his chores" on the dining room floor. Anne became very frustrated and told Grandpa to take the calf somewhere else or he and the calf would depart this earth in the same box.

CHAPTER II
Beginnings of Our Home Ranch

The large family needed a home of its own, so in 1890, Grandpa and Grandma bought one hundred and twenty acres of land originally homesteaded by Bill Huey. (Family lore says they bought the ranch to have a home for the calf.) Included in the purchase were the original two-room cabin with an attached blacksmith shop and the 1872 water right on the beautiful spring-fed stream that comes through the property. During the winter, the stream carries 3.3 cubic feet per second, and in the summer, 2.4 cubic feet per second. The water for the spring initially comes from Mount Princeton, about fifteen miles to the west of the ranch, and goes under ground and surfaces as springs in a meadow about one mile west of the ranch. The water right proved to be of immense importance for the operation of the ranch. After the original purchase, Grandpa homesteaded an adjoining forty acres to make a one hundred sixty-acre ranch. When the family moved to their new home, Dad and Uncle Bill were still in grade school and needed to walk three miles to and from the school at Nathrop. Dad never forgot he and Bill each having to carry a gun in their boots because there were freely roaming Ute Indians in the area. However, these Indians never bothered them nor anyone else in the area. Sometime later, the Indians were moved to a reservation near White Water, which was close to Grand Junction, Colorado.

In his later years, Dad often spoke about having seen the train carrying soldiers who were going to escort and assure the safety of the Indians during their move to their new site. Little did Dad know then that the commander of those soldiers would one day be his father-in-law. In gratitude for the kindness of the troops toward the Indians, the chief gave our great-grandfather a pair of baby moccasins that had been worn by the chief's son who had died. Those moccasins were a treasure in Mom's family and were displayed on the wall of their home. Sadly, years later the treasured gift disappeared from their home when Mom's last sister died.

After six years in school, Dad had "completed his books," which is probably comparable to finishing our eighth grade and left school to work on the ranch. In time Dad and Uncle Bill each homesteaded land adjacent to the original property. Finally, through the years, they acquired more land that was available either by purchase or because of unpaid taxes.

Dad and Uncle Bill built a home for Bill and his wife about a hundred yards to the north of the original cabin and Uncle Bill's homestead cabin became the bunk house. For our home, the original blacksmith shop became the kitchen. The room to which the blacksmith shop was attached became a living room and the second original room became a bedroom. After that, they raised the roof of the original cabin to make room to build two bedrooms, one for the boys and one for the girls. These rooms were built over the living room and the downstairs bedroom. The stairs from the living room to the bedrooms was enclosed. On the long side of the house, between first and second floor they attached a shelter porch to bring storm waters away from the house. The shelter porch consisted of just the roof supported by four legs. This front porch is missing today due to a peculiar, never-to-be-forgotten incident which will be explained later in this book. To complete their plans, they dug out a cellar under the living room and designed an eight by ten foot shelved, dirt cellar with an outside entrance at the living room door. The downstairs bedroom received its only heat from a wood-burning stove in the living room next door. The two bedrooms upstairs had four windows, but one in each of the two upstairs bedrooms were without glass, making those bedrooms extremely cold in the winter time. Dad wanted the windows without glass so they could be used for fire escapes, should the blowing embers from the wood stoves cause a fire in/or on the aging cabins.

Dad and Uncle Bill dug a filtering basin higher in the creek and piped the clean, filtered spring water for use on the ranch. The water from the stream was and still is used not only in the home, but for irrigation on the home meadow and cow pasture, the only two pieces of land on the property that had native hay.

CHAPTER III
Our Mother's Background

Our mother Elizabeth Ann Esser—called Libby by family and friends—was born in Cañon City, Colorado. Her mother Anna died from tuberculosis when our mother, the eldest child, was nine years old. Anna's husband Joseph Esser, our grandfather, later married his deceased wife's younger sister Amelia. Amelia never had any children of her own, but together with grandpa was a wonderful parent to the four children. When asked if she preferred her birth mother or the aunt who raised her after her mother died, Mom said she could not choose between them. She loved them both.

The family moved from Cañon City to the warden's home at the Colorado State Reformatory near Buena Vista when Grandpa Esser became deputy warden there. While living there, Grandpa, wanting to show the youngsters some "real cowboys," took them just four miles south from their new home to a ranch with cattle and cowboys. The cowboys just happened to be Dad and Uncle Bill on the Cogan Ranch. Libby, whom we always called "Mom," had German, French, and Prussian ancestors. She spoke both German and English. She became a school teacher after attending college in Greeley, Colorado. After having taught at Freegold, near the end of Trout Creek, and at Wildhorse near Buena Vista, she was hired to teach in a third one-room school on Maxwell Park. While she taught there, she boarded with neighbors a mile away from our ranch. There, as an adult, she met Dad who was about seventeen years older than she. They fell in love and married in 1918.

CHAPTER IV
Providing a Modern Home

Because rural areas had no public utilities available at that time, Dad and Uncle Bill wanted a way to have electricity on the ranch. In 1919, they purchased a generator and the gas engine that powered the generator from a prospector. The mine was at 13,000 ft. elevation on Mount Princeton. A hired team was unable to move the load down the mountain because of the steep, slippery terrain. Dad decided to try it with his favorite work horse Teddy. Dad and Uncle Bill put the total load on a homemade slip—like a low sled with logs for runners. Very slowly, Dad and Teddy made the trip down Mount Princeton by repeatedly moving a few steps and stopping to keep either horse or slip from sliding out of control. Safely the load was brought off the mountain and to the ranch. Then Dad and Bill sold the gas engine and purchased a water wheel from someone on South Lake Creek, near Leadville. They then diverted the water they needed from the creek to a ditch which came along higher on the hillside, and put in a head gate to send the water down a steep pipe to turn the water wheel which in turn powered the generator, then the water ran back into the original stream. The generator produced three kilowatts of 220-volt direct current electricity. This electricity was used to light the homes, the outside buildings, and some outdoor areas on the ranch. They had electricity on the ranch before Buena Vista, a town five miles north of the ranch, had electricity available to most homes. We also had a large electric grindstone that Dad used to sharpen everything from knives and axes to the sickles for the mowing machines. The power from the water wheel was used directly to run a large circular saw to cut logs from trees needed for corrals and ranch buildings as well as to cut the fire wood into pieces manageable for chopping. The log buildings Dad and Uncle Bill built included a slaughter house, a six-stall horse barn with a hayloft open on the sides to allow them to pitch hay directly into the feeding area of each stall, a chicken house, a brooder house, a milk house, a granary, and several cattle sheds. The corrals also had log fences. If we were in the meadow when a log was cut, we could hear the squeal of the saw above the sound of the river.

Our older family members remember professors coming from many different universities, bringing their engineering students to show them the modern miracles these sixth-grade graduates had accomplished using their ingenuity and intelligence.

A near disaster happened one day when Dad and Uncle Bill were cutting trees for logs. Dad called to Bill, "Come here, I think I broke my leg." When Uncle Bill came over to see Dad, Dad's foot was resting on his knee. Truly his leg was badly broken. To get back to the ranch, Dad had Bill put him on the lumber wagon in such a way that the broken leg was stabilized and Dad hung on until they got back to the ranch. Luckily they arrived at the ranch without Dad fainting or going into shock from his severe pain and loss of blood. Since there was no telephone on the ranch, Uncle Bill rode a horse to the nearest neighbor, a mile away, to call a doctor. Two doctors arrived, one male, and one female, both well known to the family. Placing Dad on the kitchen table, they gave him a big drink of whiskey, set his leg the best they could, and repaired the exposed tissues.

The broken leg slipped sometime later in the cast and healed in such a way that Dad always had one leg an inch and a half shorter than his other leg. Because of the large, open wound, and no available antibiotics, Dad became dangerously ill and feverish. However, in time under Mom's gentle care, the leg healed and dad could walk again. Physical therapy was unheard of at that early date. The only long-term effect was that the injury left him unable to ride a horse for long distances because it caused him too much pain.

During the summer of 1927 Dad and Uncle Bill moved Dad and Mom's homestead cabin to our home, attaching it to the other side of the then enlarged kitchen. Dad made that cabin into three rooms: a bathroom, a common walk-in family clothes closet, and a laundry room. He completed the bathroom with a toilet, bathtub, sink, electric lights, a hot water tank, and a small wood-burning stove. The new laundry room had an electric washing machine, two large stationary stone wash tubs, and an electric iron. This room also served as a pantry. One wall had a cupboard with open shelves covered with hanging curtains for storing canned, nonperishable foods, and a free-standing cupboard with a door and shelves for day-to-day foods. Mom used one of the laundry tubs, when not being used for laundry, to keep our milk, cottage cheese, butter, and small amounts of meal leftovers cool. She did this by placing the inner part of an old ice box with shelves on a raised platform in the bottom of one stationary tub. She laid dish towels over the waterproof top and down both sides of the box. The two tubs shared one water tap via a hose. Mom put the hose on top of the box and let a trickle of cold water keep the cloths wet as the water dripped into the tub. This unique contraption kept our food cool so none would spoil. Years later when they could afford to buy blocks of ice, they got an old used ice box. They purchased their first refrigerator in 1950 after most of us had left home.

The two upstairs bedrooms were cold in winter. We slept two to a bed to help keep us warm. Mom made duck feather comforters for each bed and when temperatures hovered between twenty to forty degrees below zero, she placed wrapped heated bricks in our beds to make them warm for us when we retired. How well I remember undressing downstairs by the stove and dashing upstairs to my bed. When I got up in the morning, I ran to dress near the stove in the downstairs room.

Our Mom, a city girl, learned to do all the many things a rancher's wife needed to know. She excelled in everything she attempted. She baked, cooked, and made needed clothing, sheets, and pillow cases from the sacks in which we had purchased flour, sugar, and chicken feed. Later, when we girls were growing older, she made our school and Sunday dresses which we proudly wore. In those days, we girls never wore ranch blue jeans or overalls when we went into town. Mom canned meat from deer and our cattle because she had no place to freeze anything. She also canned fruit which we bought, and vegetables from our own large garden. She did these things while still taking care of the daily needs of the large family. When we were old enough we worked in the garden and helped prepare the food for the table or to be canned. My favorite job was to lay out the rows and to plant the garden. Mom helped with the planning and oversaw the planting. The other siblings stayed out of the way until weeding time. They also learned how to turn the water from the ditch into the rows to water the plants without flooding anything. One side of the garden, along the main ditch, had rhubarb plants and current bushes. The rhubarb was canned and the currents made into wonderful jelly. The other side of the garden where water would drain from the rows, had raspberry bushes. We ate the raspberries as they ripened.

In the early years, summer grazing for cattle was on the open range. In late September and early October, Dad would be gone about a month to ride with the other ranchers in the yearly cattle roundup. They gathered the cows from thousands of grazing acres and branded the calves. At the end of the roundup they separated the animals into herds with matching brands. Then each rancher had his own cows and calves to take home. These times were difficult for Mom, because she had to be both mother and father to her growing family during Dad's absence.

Just before the "crash" in 1929, Dad purchased 190 acres of hay meadows three miles south of the home ranch. When the "crash" hit there was no incoming money to pay for the land because when our cattle were shipped to Denver to be sold, the income was not enough even to pay the freight on the shipment and in addition, we had a year's supply of grocery bills which had to be paid. Dad borrowed money from a bank in Salida, using the ranch as collateral. The Bank carried our family's debt through the depression until the late 1940s when it was fully paid. Our youngest brother Joe met the banker years later, thanked him, and asked why he had permitted the Cogan's to have an outstanding debt for so many years. The banker said, "I trusted that the loan would be repaid, and anyway I would never have known how to care for a ranch."

Dad and Uncle Bill, these two hard working Irishmen, cared for their wives and children, did everything on the ranch themselves, and yet were always ready to help their neighboring ranchers with their animals and buildings as well as supporting them with asked-for advice about both personal and ranching matters. When they needed help they could count on neighbors also.

CHAPTER V
The Children

Amelia: From Birth to Convent

On February 12, 1919, the first baby, Amelia Anne, arrived. She was a tiny, premature infant born at home. Dad's mother Anna helped a nurse with the delivery. Because Amelia was very small, weighing a little over four pounds, and the winter was cold, she needed a warm crib. The special incubator which she occupied was a shoebox kept on the oven door of the wood-burning kitchen stove to provide warmth during the day. (Amelia, now Sister Leann, says this is the reason she is half-baked.) At night, she slept with Mom and Dad. Although premature, Amelia thrived and grew to be a strong and healthy child. Because Amelia was born during the flu epidemic, the family remained isolated on the ranch until the danger was past. The new baby is now known as Sister Leann. Amelia will be used in this book until the point at which officially she becomes Sister Leander.

At the age of two and a half years, Amelia had a near fatal case of erysipelas (a bacterial skin infection). The doctor told the nurse to burn rings with strong carbolic acid around her waist and above her knees to keep the infection from spreading.

Leann's Story—In Her Own Words

I have scars even today because the rinse which was supposed to neutralize the acid was ineffective, and I suffered severe burns. I had to remain in bed for six weeks. I remember very clearly, the first time Mom carried me outside in her arms to show me the rock lined ditch with flowing water in our front yard. That beautiful sight made me feel well again. Even today as an adult, I can honestly say that my education about extreme pain had begun at that early age.

During this time, my first baby brother, John (Jack), was born, and I was no longer the center of attraction, but I loved Jack very much and adjusted well. In two more years, another baby brother, Jerry, arrived. I was very happy being the eldest and able to help care for my younger brothers. When Jack was old enough to talk, he decided it was easier to speak in some type of simple, unknown language saying words like "lop la la." Jack knew I understood him and I talked for him. I found out very soon that he could speak clearly for himself. He just knew he got more attention with his lazy language, and I soon quit translating for him.

When I was five years old, my dad's mother Anna died of pneumonia. Jack, baby Jerry, and I were taken to a friend to be cared for until the funeral was over. Jack and I had never seen Dad cry, and seeing him cry then was very painful for us. Both Jack and I loved her because she had been such a kind and loving grandmother.

What I loved to do was climb. By the time I was five years old, I could climb the log corral fences and many trees. Finally, as a real test, I climbed a tall light pole. How defeated I felt when a young neighbor man had to rescue me because I was afraid to slide down the pole alone.

When I was in the first grade I got to be a snowflake in a school play. My self-esteem was left in shambles when one of the boys said to me, "You cannot be just a snowflake because you are a whole snowdrift!" I assume this remark came from the fact that I was stout, muscular, and energetic—very unlike a dainty, slowly drifting snowflake.

Being the eldest, I became very active always wanting to do my best in many activities. The one indoor activity in which I never did well was playing the piano. After taking piano lessons, I made my disastrous, first public performance. I trembled so badly that I could not find even one correct key on the piano. Because of this, my teacher informed me that I could never become a pianist, thus ending my piano lessons. This tragedy made me happy because that meant I could be outdoors much more instead of practicing my piano lessons.

Even in my very earliest years, I would bring in all the horses from the pasture, saddle, and ride them. Dad showed me how to harness a team of work horses for use in the fields. One great lesson I learned was that one must never unhook all the many buckles on the harnesses. When I brought my team in from the field for the first time, I undid all the buckles on the entire harness, much to Dad's dismay. However, I learned my lesson quickly.

Dad also taught me to safely handle and shoot a gun, but for safety reasons I always hunted rabbits alone on our many acres of hills and valleys. The rabbits I killed I was responsible to dress and clean to make them ready for baking. I also loved the many hours I spent fishing on the Arkansas River, in our creek, and the meadow ditches. I became an expert as a fly-fishing youngster. Yes, being the eldest in the family, I could have been termed an independent, classical tomboy.

One day, Mom had some leftover pancake dough, and I tried to give it to a bridled horse in the front yard, instead of giving it to the chickens, as I had been told. The poor horse could not swallow with the bit in his mouth, so Dad came to rectify the situation by unbridling the horse. What was special in our family and what we even today appreciate remembering, is that in our learning difficulties, Dad and Mom were never upset about our many mistakes but always kindly taught us to do things in a better or correct way.

From my view at the top of the corral fences, I was fascinated watching the men brand and dehorn the calves. I also did my share of helping Dad and Uncle Bill when they butchered our cows. The meat was used for our food as well as to help pay for our grocery bills. My job was not easy and never very appetizing, but I swept the butchered cow's blood into the drainage gutter, which emptied into an outside container.

Our special neighbor lady Georgie had a wealthy guest, a doctor's wife, from St. Louis, Missouri. Georgie brought this guest to the ranch as she needed someone to help the guest zip up her corset. I was strong and able to do things quickly and was thrilled to be asked to help. However, not realizing it, I zipped not only the corset but also the skin and flesh as well. After she screamed, it took both Mom and Georgie to free this nice lady and care for the wounds.

In my younger years, the Abbot at Holy Cross Abbey in Cañon City, Colorado, came to see Mom and Dad. He had with him a white mother and her two half Indian sons. The Abbot said it would be wrong to have the three in jail awaiting the mother's trial for murdering her Indian husband. He asked our parents to take the three of them to live at the ranch with us where they would be safe and cared for in a kindly way. Naturally, I enjoyed behaving like an Indian in trying "to keep ahead" of these guests. When the woman was acquitted, the family was then able to move away. Losing those wonderful friends made me extremely sad.

I attended the public grade and high school in Buena Vista, Colorado, about five miles away from home. Since there was no school bus transportation and Dad couldn't take time away from his work to drive us to and from school, I was given a special permit at age fourteen to be our dependable chauffeur. This permit was restricted to just the route between the ranch and school. After I graduated, the eldest school-aged family member drove to school. While being able to drive to school, we were never allowed to drive any other place until each of us was old enough to have a legal driver's license. During those years, gasoline was expensive, costing eleven cents a gallon. Dad gave me strict orders never to drive more than thirty-two miles an hour to save gasoline. Also, our 1929 Model A Ford shimmied every time I happened to break the assigned speed limit.

I played basketball on the Buena Vista High School's Demon Team. I was a strong athlete and played well. Once when I was guarding a smaller player, the girl pretended to throw the ball over my head. I jumped high hoping to catch the ball, but at the same time, the smaller girl ran with the ball between my legs. Dad was watching the game and told me that I looked for the ball, but not being able to locate it, I became puzzled since I was certain the ball had gone over my head. My team competed and won many games at schools even in other counties of the state. I relished the competition in those games and learned to be both a good winner as well as a good loser.

Dad built us a wonderful, but muddy, swimming pond that was full of cold spring water from our creek. I learned to swim and was responsible for keeping my younger siblings safe while in the water. Swimming was one of my greatest gifts. One day our family went to a Sunday School picnic at Mount Princeton Hot Springs, a commercial, heated pool. During the activity, I became aware my younger brother Jack was struggling in the deepest end of the pool. No one else noticed his dilemma, but thankfully I could swim and saved him from drowning.

All the younger siblings learned to ski under my tutelage. Our skis had just a toe strap, and we never had ski poles, so balance was extremely necessary for us to enjoy this sport. I made a ski course about two hundred yards long. It started on the hill north of our house, came down between the trees and the rabbit hutches, continued down over a rock-lined irrigation ditch, under the clothes line, and down the slope toward the highway fence where we had to stop. Most of us just fell to escape running into the fence. We used a great amount of energy climbing many times a day to the top of our ski course, but never did we complain because we enjoyed every minute of exercise, while we shared in the great fun.

When I was in high school, I got to help Dad, Uncle Bill, and Bill's son, Bill Jr., drive our cattle herd up State Highway 285 on the way to our summer grazing pastures in the high altitude of the national forest. Traveling about thirty-five miles on the highway was difficult because of people in cars wishing to take pictures of the horses and their riders disturbed the safe movement of the cattle. Those of us on horses tried to move the herd along in a sensible way making a path for the cars, thus keeping the animals and car passengers safe. (Often I had heard Dad tell of one drive when someone in an expensive, very shiny car was determined to get a close-up picture of two bulls fighting. Dad told them that was dangerous and to please move on. They persisted until one bull saw his reflection in the car door and charged into the side of the car, doing a lot of damage. Yes, then they followed orders and got out of there.) After the highway trek and one night of rest, the cattle had to be driven nearly two more days and one more night to reach their summer grazing lands in the high Rocky Mountains. These were very difficult days for everyone, especially for Dad because with his leg problem, he had to walk a lot of the time. Since I had ridden horses often enough not to have sore legs, and I was also young and healthy, I enjoyed every moment of these drives. In the fall, we brought the cattle home via the same long drive.

When I graduated from Buena Vista High School, I received a scholarship to Mount St. Scholastica College in Atchison, Kansas. I have one vivid memory from that time. I was having some digestive problems. Someone gave me an Alka-Seltzer. Since I had never even seen one of those tablets, I bit into it and took a drink of water. One of the other girls could not believe her eyes when I started foaming copiously from the mouth. She kindly assisted me as I got rid of the foaming mess and rinsed my mouth.

After three semesters in college, I entered Mount St. Scholastica, Convent which was situated on the same campus. There I became Sister Leander. Years later I shortened and feminized my name to Sister Leann.

The Birth of John and a Short Sketch of His Life

The first Cogan son was born on June 30, 1921, on the ranch. He was named John after our dad, but at home we always called him Jack. Because he had severe hay fever, he could not tolerate the hay and weeds that grew around home so when he was young, he spent summers with our maternal grandparents in Cañon City. When he was old enough to tend the cattle on the summer range, he lived with a prospector up Pine Creek and looked after the cattle. His stories from those summers would make a book by themselves and to hear him tell them is a real treat.

After graduating from Buena Vista High School, he went to college at Colorado School of Mines in Golden, Colorado. Because some of the perquisite classes were not offered in Buena, he studied them by himself when he got to the School of Mines. When World War II started, he and a few other engineering students at the college were drafted into the army, but in a very short time Jack, with one or two others of that group, were moved into the Marines as commissioned officers. He spent most of his time during the Second World War in the South Pacific areas. After VJ Day, he was sent to Hiroshima, Japan, as an engineer to help with the necessary building after the bombing.

There he spent his free time visiting and playing with children in a nearby orphanage which was run by Catholic sisters.

John (Jack) had a rank of Captain when he received his honorable discharge. When he returned to the states he went back to Colorado School of Mines where he finished his Master of Engineering degree. While studying in Golden, he met and married Sally Forster, a nurse working in Denver. They lived most of their married lives in Texas where Jack worked for Shell Oil Company. Jack and Sally raised six children, one girl and five boys. Sally worked as a nurse but was also an accomplished seamstress. She made most of their family clothes. Her sewing ability was shown most definitely in her own beautiful wedding dress. As their family grew she kept a record with many photographs, then with grandchildren, many more photographs. She died January 7, 2000, just months before she and Jack would have celebrated their 50th wedding anniversary. After Sally's death, Jack moved back to Salida, Colorado. There he enjoyed fishing almost daily, until, because of ill health, he moved to Colorado Springs. Presently, Jack lives in an assisted living facility here in Colorado Springs. You will hear more of Jack and Sally in remembrances of early life on the ranch in later chapters.

The Birth of Jeremiah and a Short Sketch of His Life

The second son was born on November 25, 1922, on the ranch. He was named Jeremiah after Dad's father. He was always known as Jerry. Because he was still on the ranch when World War II broke out, he was deferred from military service because of Dad's need for him on the ranch. Amelia and Jack had both left home by the time Jerry graduated from high school. Jerry married Vivian Yates. Vivian was a loving wife and mother. Being a person of many talents, she used those talents generously for family and others.

After the birth of the ninth of their eleven children, they moved to Fairbanks, Alaska, where they hoped to homestead. For a while they lived in a Quonset hut, with hanging sheets dividing the area into rooms. Besides supporting their family by working at a dairy, Jerry used his free time to locate enough land without permafrost for their homestead. He found the place they wanted, and he built their home. Some of the boys were old enough by that time to help with the building and learned much in the process. Jerry spoke often of trudging alone through very deep snow in the dark from the main road to the homestead house after work at the dairy because, even during the winter, he was required to sleep at the homestead to fulfill the government regulations for claiming title to the land. After school was out in the spring, the entire family lived at the homestead. They cultivated land so they could have a garden and a potato patch. Neighbors who were invited to share the large potato patch, helped with the planting and the harvesting. Between those times, Jerry and the family kept the potatoes watered and hilled. In time Jerry built a large log home in Fairbanks where they lived during the school year because the children's education was a high priority.

While living in Fairbanks and vicinity, their family increased to eleven children, eight boys and three girls. These grown children are now parents and grandparents themselves. The complete story of this "frontier" family would itself make an exciting book. Vivian died July 27, 2012 and Jerry died February 23, 2013. You will hear more about Jerry and Vivian in remembrances of early life on the ranch in later chapters.

The Birth of Mary Margaret and a Short Sketch of Her Life

The first girl to be born after Amelia was named Mary Margaret. She was born on June 28, 1927, in Salida, Colorado. She grew up with her older family members and was special not only to those older than she, but also to her two younger sisters, Kathleen and Beth, and her youngest brother, Joe.

When Mary Margaret graduated from Buena Vista High School, she received a scholarship to Mount St. Scholastica College in Atchison, Kansas. After one year of college there, she entered St. Joseph School of Nursing in Denver, Colorado, and became a registered nurse. As a nurse, she worked in Salida, at the Denver and Rio Grande Railroad Hospital. She fell in love and married Norman Eggleston, a cattle rancher from the area. They had six children, four girls and two boys.

Norman had been a spotter pilot in the Army during World War II. Despite having been shot down over enemy territory, he came home unharmed. He worked hard to keep the ranch going and, in time, his sons were old enough to help him. He was a very kind, gentle, patient man. Their original home was west of Salida, on a level with the Arkansas River. Later, they built a home on higher ground in the same area. When they retired, they sold the ranch and moved to Salida. Mary Margaret lost her beloved husband Norman on June 23, 2011, in their 60th year of marriage.

She presently lives alone in her home where her adult family members and their spouses, her grandchildren, and greatgrandchildren spend time with her on weekends and during vacations. Despite using a cane and being unable to stoop over because of a mended broken back, she tends her beautiful flower garden and vegetable garden throughout spring and summer. She enjoys her fresh produce from the earliest lettuce and radishes to the last carrot before frost comes. In addition, whatever harvest can be stored or frozen is safely put away for the winter months, except what the squirrels make off with for their winter store. You will read more about Mary Margaret and Norman in remembrances in later chapters.

Kathleen: From Birth to Convent

The fifth child to arrive in the Cogan household was named Kathleen. She was born in Salida, Colorado, on February 4, 1929. Having four older siblings, she was the center of attention and greatly loved, causing some struggles in deciding who got to hold her.

Kathleen's Story—In Her Own Words

When I was very young, but able to be outside alone, I discovered an old, well chewed ham bone belonging to the dog and cats. All children need to taste things new to them, and I was no exception, so I evidently chewed on the bone myself. Sometime later, I spiked a high fever and had a seizure. Mom, who always knew what to do, immediately put me in cold water in a tub. I survived without any ill effects. Sister Leann clearly remembers how frightened she was seeing all this happen to me.

As a three- or four-year-old, one day I was unable to get into my bathing suit quickly enough to go to our swimming hole with the others. I had tangled myself in the top net portion of my suit and could not even free myself. There was no choice for me except to go to Uncle Bill who was caring for us while our parents were gone. He was in the kitchen hand turning a large barrel churn to make butter. I remember even today how embarrassed I was to have anyone except Mom totally undress me. He took off my suit, straightened it, and put it on so I could happily run off to go swimming.

Before I was old enough to go to school, my sister Mary Margaret taught me many things a first grader needed to know. Therefore, when I started school, I was soon moved to the second grade, just one class below Mary Margaret.

Still deeply embedded in my memory is the fact that because I was the smallest girl in school at that time, l was chosen to be the special angel in the Christmas play. I remember Mom telling me how beautiful I was that evening on the stage even though I had noticeably bowed legs.

My siblings soon nicknamed me, "Calamity Jane," because I was always the first one getting out of the car and racing into the house after school, so I could be first to tell Mom, and anyone else who would listen, all the news of the day that I had heard and all about my experiences at school.

When we needed to carry lunches to school we always had Mom's delicious homemade bread for peanut butter and jelly sandwiches and graham crackers decorated with chocolate frosting. One morning, Mom asked me to frost the graham crackers. Finding no powdered sugar, I just hurriedly substituted flour, and mixed it with the powered cocoa. What a mess! That meant we ate plain crackers that day.

I was a second grader when the old building we were in was closed and we all moved to our new school in what had been the Chaffee County courthouse. This was much better as we had a four-acre playground with swings, a merry-go-round, and a baseball field. At noon break however, I preferred going with some of the other students over the low fence on the north side of the playground. There we played over and around the huge rocks which were wonderful places for us to climb and hide from each other. I enjoyed every minute we played, but for me, as a smaller student, when the school bell rang, I always had a difficult time keeping up with my friends in running back to school on time.

Our family had one or two pairs of roller skates. They were the kind that needed to be attached to the soles of our shoes, using a skate key for tightening them. For many recesses and sometimes after school Mary Margaret and I skated on the long sidewalks around the school, as we had no place to skate at home.

Speaking of roller skates, our entire family went sometimes to Cañon City to visit our grandparents and other relatives. The trip in our Model T truck usually took between two and three hours one way. I loved going there because I loved my grandparents and we didn't get to see them very often. One day I decided to roller skate around the block. After skating for a while, I could not find my grandparent's home, because every home looked just like theirs. When I did not return at a reasonable time, my older siblings were sent to find me. I was still skating, but was lost and extremely frightened. I was overjoyed when they found me.

Another time when we were in Cañon City, our maternal grandfather's brother, Uncle Bill Esser, offered those of us who were old enough to tour the Colorado State Penitentiary where he worked as a prison guard. I remember that several of us, probably then in the upper grades, were the lucky ones, or so we thought. Uncle Bill took us through the main portion of the prison to the outside yard in the back, still within the high prison fence. He offered to let us walk "The Last Mile" to the building where they gassed the death row prisoners. There he permitted each of us who wished, to sit in the gas chamber chair. Being the youngest of the group, I was one of those who volunteered. I wasn't exactly thrilled at the time, but this excursion furnished an everlasting memory for me. It made me certain that I would never do anything bad which would cause me to be in prison.

Each year, in the early spring our parents ordered two hundred female baby chicks. To prepare a safe place for these tiny chicks, Dad always fumigated the old log brooder house to get rid of any bugs, spiders or fleas. I clearly remember the odor of the fumigant which smelled like peach seeds. After the poison was well aired out of the building, Dad lighted the kerosene brooder stove to keep the room toasty warm for the chicks.

The baby chicks would arrive in Buena by train in the early afternoon. We had to leave school immediately to take them home. With the chicks in their boxes, we all sat around the kitchen table to give each chick two drinks of water. This was necessary because since the chicks had not had water during the train trip, they needed it immediately. We held each one gently in one hand and with the other hand we carefully moved their head so their beak touched the water. When they had twice put their beaks up above their heads to swallow, we knew they were safe to take to the warm brooder house.

On some school days, if the car had been needed at the ranch, we waited in the safe, warm, post office for our only car to come from the ranch. Very quickly I learned how to open every mailbox by using the two secret safety numbers on each mailbox. I learned to do that by listening for different cliques. I enjoyed those challenges until I told Mom of my wonderfully, great accomplishments. She quickly put an end to my fun.

The Fourth of July each year, Dad taught each of us how to shoot a twenty-two rifle for target practice and taught us the necessary safety issues. I was too small the first time, so I needed to rest my gun on a saw horse. I became a good shot, but even when I became older, I never hunted any animals, like Amelia and my older brothers did, but was thrilled to know how to safely handle and shoot a gun.

The most difficult remembrance of my early school days pertained to an elderly, kind cobbler, Chris Hamdorf. Whenever we family members needed our only pair of shoes soled, heeled, or repaired in any way, we went after school to his shop. There we got to sit, visit with him, and watch him repair our shoes. Chris was a wise and true friend of mine.

Chris died in his shop and was not found for a few days. Knowing Chris had no relatives, our parents asked those of us who were older to attend his afternoon funeral. The only thing I remember was seeing him in his coffin with extremely red hands and face. He was the first deceased person I had ever seen. That sight haunted me for a long time, especially when I needed to go alone into our barn to gather the chicken eggs from under the grain boxes in the dark horse stalls.

The most embarrassing situation in my teenage life happened when I was a senior in high school. One day when I was in a study hall being supervised by the principal, the principal's office telephone rang. The principal asked me to go answer it. I went into his office but had never seen nor used a phone attached to the wall, nor even a desk phone. I looked and looked at the ringing phone hoping someone would come by to help me, but no one came. I had to go back to my principal and tell him I didn't know how to answer the phone. He couldn't believe that I had never seen nor used a phone! Immediately, he took me to the office and gave me lessons on answering, dialing, and generally how to use a phone.

One of the important happenings was the time Amelia was left at home to take care of us younger siblings. Mary Margaret and I were fussing about something and Amelia, to settle us, took us upstairs to bed. I chose to go to the boy's bedroom in which there were old magazines on the stand by the bed. Amelia gave me strict orders not to even touch the magazines. When Amelia went downstairs, naturally I took a magazine to read. Shortly thereafter, I heard footsteps on the stairs. Instead of placing the magazine back from where I had taken it, I shoved it under the blankets. Amelia arrived, pulled back the blankets and there was the magazine! Knowing I was in real trouble, I jumped out of the bed slipped around Amelia and ran downstairs, out the door and along the side of the house to where the corner porch leg had the attached wire fence of the front lawn stretched from that leg to the corner of the house. I knew if I jumped that section of fence, I would be scot free. But I caught my toe in the top wire, down I went onto the lawn, and down came the entire porch! Although I had a hard fall, I was not physically injured, but there was disaster behind me. We were fearful to have our parents return to see the catastrophe. When they did return, Dad, seeing the mess, said to Mom, "Libby, didn't we have a porch when we left?" We culprits explained what had happened, and since neither was injured, we were not punished. Our younger sister Beth, remembers having heard our parents discussing the incident later. They said that they had known the porch was old and dangerous. They had already made plans to take it down and not replace it when I had brought it down by one errant jump. The permanent scar on the side of the house was an obvious clue that there had once been a porch. Even paint could not hide it. That scar remained visible for many years until our younger brother Joe and his wife Arlene had siding installed on the house.

In the early spring and summer, the melting snow from the higher elevations made the Arkansas River much higher and very muddy. This caused some of the river water to back up in the drainage ditches in our meadow. These ditches then provided safe and favorite places away from the river for us younger family members to fish and catch nice large river fish. One day Beth, Joe, and I were fishing in one of these ditches. The fish were not biting, because they had seen us, and had gone to hide under the banks. I decided to catch some with my hands. This was against the law, and was also extremely difficult, as the fish were strong and slippery. Getting on my tummy on the grass next to the ditch, I slipped my hands under the bank. Immediately I yelled, "I have a big one!" The only problem was that instead of pulling out a fish, I pulled out a big, long, bull snake. It scared me so badly that I screamed, dropped the snake, and ran all the way home.

Another thing Mary Margaret and I decided to do was to smoke like our older cousin, Bill, who lived on the ranch with his parents. He always easily and expertly rolled his own cigarettes. There were weeds on the ranch we called "Indian tobacco" since the seeds looked just like real tobacco. We two girls hid behind the barn, the most dangerous place on the ranch for fire. We rolled two cigarettes just like Bill did except we had to use toilet paper in the absence of real cigarette paper. We even licked the edges to be sure no tobacco would escape. Lighting our wonderful prizes with matches was easy. Each of us took one, big whiff. The smoke was terrible and we became nauseous and coughed for a long time. What a mistake that was! We quickly dug a hole and hid our evidence. Neither of us smoked again during our entire lifetimes.

When Mary Margaret and I were old enough, we got to feed the weaned milk cow calves their milk from buckets. The calves were kept in a small, log corral and always came readily for their suppers. I decided it would be fun to ride one. That worked well for several evenings until one dumped me in a pile of fresh manure. I was absolutely frightened, decorated as I was, to go back to the house since we had been told never to even try to ride the calves.

Mary Margaret and I went horseback riding in open pasture land west of the ranch. We were enjoying the beautiful day, close to the mountain range in all its beauty. All at once my horse, Kate, began to run. Kate had originally been used as a race horse before being purchased by our family. I tried my best to stop her, but the saddle cinch loosened, and my saddle blankets fell to the ground. My jacket, which was tied behind the saddle, also went flying. The saddle was loose enough that it could have dumped me to the ground. Not being able to even make her slow down, I hung on for dear life. After Kate had run a great distance, me pulling the reins with all my strength, I finally got her stopped. I was totally exhausted and frightened. We tightened the cinch then headed for home, picking up the coat and saddle blankets where they had fallen.

Another time Beth, Joe, and I rode horses along the highway just to enjoy the ride one beautiful day. Joe picked up an old tire inner tube with which he planned to make sling shots for his beanies, which he used for shooting rocks. The day went well until we arrived at the fence of the lawn in front of our house. When I got off my horse, I wound the reins of the bridle around a fence post, and stooped over next to the horse to put on my overshoes. At that very moment, Joe threw the tire inner tube on the ground next to my horse. This frightened her, and when she reared, she pulled out several fence posts from the ground which were still attached to the fence. The entire mess of posts and fence went over my head since I was still bent down. After getting loose from enough wire to be able to get back on her feet, the frightened horse kept moving backwards down the hill toward the creek. She moved in erratic ways, making the one post still attached to the reins keep swinging over her head causing her to become more frightened. None of us knew what to do, but luckily Dad was in the house, and hearing the noise, came immediately to help. He moved very slowly toward the horse, kept calling her by name, thus calming her. Gently touching her head, he continued to call her by name. The tangled horse then permitted Dad to carefully free her from the torn fence and the fence posts. This was an exceedingly frightening experience for everyone. Luckily no one including the horse was injured. Dad had a special relationship with our horses and all the ranch animals. He always treated them compassionately and with real love. His gentleness with them formed a special trust between him and them. He was really, "an exceedingly good shepherd."

I graduated from Buena Vista High School and received a scholarship to Mount Saint Scholastica College in Atchison, Kansas. The wonderful sisters teaching in the college were excellent role models for us. While there, I was one of a few students unable to go home for the Thanksgiving holidays. During one of these holidays, I decided to scare my classmate Noreen who had also stayed at the college. I turned out the dormitory lights and hid inside the door planning to scare her when she came to go to bed. I heard footsteps coming to the door and jumped out just in time to catch her. However, to my surprise, I had caught Sister Imogene, my dormitory supervisor, around the legs, habit, and all. How embarrassed I was! Luckily, Sister Imogene thought it was funny, so I was not even scolded.

I studied there in Atchison for one year, then chose to go into St. Joseph School of Nursing in Denver where Mary Margaret was in her second year. I had finished two years of a three-year nursing program there when I entered the convent in Atchison, Kansas, next to where I had spent my first year of college.

There I became Sister Mary Lambert, at least for many years. Eventually I went back to my baptismal name, Sister Kathleen.

Elizabeth: From Birth to Convent

Our youngest sister, Elizabeth, was born in Salida, Colorado, on August 2, 1932. She was a tiny, blue-eyed, blond beauty, and again all her older brothers and sisters had to take their special turns to hold and love her. Even when she was an infant, she was called "Beth" because we had two other persons on the ranch who were named Elizabeth. These were our Mother, "Libby," and Uncle Bill's wife, "Aunt Lizzie." Before Beth left home our cousin Bill's new wife was also "Elizabeth Cogan."

Beth was the sedate one in our family. She had and still has a quiet sense of humor with which she entertains family and guests. She has kept in her memory many entertaining incidents she has witnessed as well as many jokes she has heard.

Piano lessons were a wonderful gift for her. She took lessons from a retired teacher in exchange for our ranch eggs. She also learned to play the old treadle organ in church. She has a clear high soprano voice and is also able to sing alto if needed. Even now, at the age of eighty-five, she often cantors for our prayers and sometimes cantors by herself at our Sunday masses.

Beth's fifth grade teacher taught both girls and boys to knit. During World War II, they knitted and stitched together squares for an afghan for the military. Throughout her life she has used that gift to knit or to crochet numerous baby sweaters with hoods, adult sweaters, two Irish knit bedspreads, and afghans. Presently, she is crocheting beautiful afghans of various patterns and sizes for the poor from yarn which individuals have had left over from their projects.

Elizabeth's Story—In Her Own Words

My first story is a about my being on center stage when I was too young to remember, but our family members delight in telling it. We had been to Salida on a hot summer day and came home in the late afternoon without having had anything to eat. Our family made beer, mostly to be used during the haying season. That hot day they enjoyed a beer before their evening meal. Evidently, I ran around and got a sip of each person's beer. When the family sat down to eat, they say I was "higher than a kite." I laughed loudly and mashed my potatoes with my fists, entertaining everyone except Mom, who let everyone know if that ever happened again, all the home brew would go in the creek. Believe me, it never happened again. "

When I was given my first prized toothbrush, my little brother Joe used my coveted possession to brush his teeth in the toilet. What a disaster for me because I couldn't understand why Mom burned my toothbrush. When Mom bought me a new toothbrush, I kept it hidden in the bathroom cupboard where Joe could not find it.

School years were hard for me. The older family members had shown great mental abilities. As a Cogan, the teachers expected me to excel. Learning came very slowly and painfully for me. My gift was that once I understood something, I retained it, but the process took time.

I was a spindly, skinny girl when I entered the first grade, but by the time I was ten years old, I weighed over one hundred pounds. This is evidenced by the fact that as a fourth grader, I was chosen to be Papa Bear, in "Goldie Locks and the Three Bears." The heavier I got, the crankier I got. World War II was being fought and my aunt dubbed me "The War Department." Finally, a doctor diagnosed my problem as hypothyroidism. With the thyroid medicine, my weight problem remained, but my disposition improved greatly.

When I was in the fifth grade, Mrs. Roman, our music teacher, taught us to dance. Boys lined up on one side of the gym and the girls on the other side. Each one's partner would be the one standing directly across the gym. We learned the waltz, "Put Your Little Foot," and the square dance—which included taking turns to call the square dances. It was fun because dances were the main entertainment throughout the Valley, and everyone young and old danced. One day in class I had a partner who was much shorter and thinner than I. He kept bumping me into other couples. Mrs. Roman stopped playing the piano and said, "Boys, if you can't see over the girl's shoulder, look around her."

My partner stepped back and said in all seriousness. "Mrs. Roman, what do I do? I can't see over Beth and I can't see around her!"

He did not get an answer. Mrs. Roman turned and began to play the piano again with much vigor. No doubt she was too full of giggles to answer him.

We had a German man, Frank, hired to care for the cattle on the summer range. He would come periodically to get supplies and visit with Dad about the cattle and other news. One day when he came, Mom wasn't home. I was probably twelve or thirteen years old. He asked me to make him a cup of coffee—this was in the days long before "instant" coffee. Mom was the only one in our family who would drink coffee so she made herself one cup every morning, and unless company came, that was all for the day. I told him that I did not know how to make coffee but that everything was right there and he was welcome to make his own, but he still insisted.

"Every woman knows how to make coffee. You make it." And I did, making sure it was strong enough for a man. He drank it and said nothing, but the next time he came, I happened to be alone again. He asked if he could make coffee.

He said, "You are right, you do not know how to make coffee. When I got to the hills, after I drank your coffee, I had to get off my horse and sit under a tree because I was so dizzy."

Money was short, but we never suffered from it. We had our own meat, eggs, milk and garden vegetables and when fruit was in season, we also canned that. What we bought at the grocery store went on a bill. In the fall when the yearlings were sold, the first part of the check went toward the debt on the ranch, then for the grocery bills. If there wasn't enough money to pay the entire bills, Dad and Uncle Bill butchered cattle to complete the payments. Small items like school supplies, we paid for from the money we got selling eggs. We knew we did not have money to spend like some other families, but we were never burdened with hearing about our mortgage on the ranch.

One day when I was a senior in high school, Mom was extremely happy and when I questioned her about her being so happy, she replied, "Your Dad just went to the bank and paid the last of the debt on the ranch!" As Dad was fifty-four when I was born, he was well into his seventies when the debt was paid in full.

When our horses were no longer able to be used for driving cattle, we kept them in the home pastures. Those were the horses we young ones could ride whenever we wanted. Usually we walked farther to find them in the hills or meadow than we rode, but anyway it gave us time and freedom to ride. One day Kathleen and I had an elderly, gentle horse named Fashion. Kathleen was in the saddle and I was behind the saddle. Kathleen wanted to go through a patch of cactus. Fashion had other ideas and went over to the bushes at the base of a hillside covered with pinion trees. She stopped beside a medium-sized bush and would not move. As we tried to urge her on with our heels, the saddle turned and we both tumbled into the bush which was a much softer landing than the cactus patch would have been. The cinch had become loose, which we didn't know, but Fashion had felt it and took care of us. Kathleen was most unhappy with me because I didn't need to fall as I was behind the saddle, but I had hung onto her and fell with her anyway. Then I refused to get back on the horse at all. She rode and I walked the rest of the way home.

When I was in high school, I played the organ at church. One day when I was on my way to get the car to go to Buena Vista to play for a wedding, a carload of Benedictine nuns from Antonito on their way to Denver, stopped to use the bathroom. I just greeted them and went on. Years later I was missioned with one of those sisters.

One day she said to me, "I met one of your sisters—the big fat one—when we stopped by your ranch. I don't remember her name, but she was a big fat one and was leaving home to play the organ for a wedding." I laughed and told her I was the big fat one, now fifty pounds lighter. When she finally believed me, she was very embarrassed.

My most embarrassing moment came one day when I was in high school. My sister-in-law, Vivian, and I were in our bathroom. There was only one bathroom in the house, but an outhouse on the hill behind the house was used for emergencies since we were a big family. Vivian was curling her hair and I was visiting with her. Joe came knocking at the door. I told him we were busy, to go up the hill. Usually when this happened to him, and I was the one in the bathroom, he would pile the broom, mop, and anything else he could lay his hands on against the door so everything would fall at my feet when I opened the door to come out. I was surprised to open the door with no landslide. As I came into the kitchen, someone was standing close by. Without looking I assumed it was Joe. I bowed way down so my long hair swept the floor and said, "There your majesty, you can get in there." I looked up into the face of a perfectly strange man. He looked surprised and I ran back into the bathroom. We had a sign on the road that we sold fresh eggs and this gentleman had stopped to buy some. Joe was in the other room packing eggs for the man. When Joe came into the kitchen with the eggs, the man, looking very confused said, "What was that?" Joe, having not seen what I had done, was unable to answer. To my knowledge, the startled man never came back to buy eggs again.

When Joe and I were in high school, our brother, Jack was serious about a nurse he had met and was dating in Denver. In Golden, at the Colorado School of Mines, Jack was finishing his engineering degree work which had been interrupted by his being drafted into the military during World War II. He was planning to bring his intended, Sally, and her mother to the ranch to get acquainted. Although he brought them, he couldn't stay because he had to go back to his college classes. Before their coming, Jack got Joe and me together to give us instructions on how to behave properly when Sally and her mother would be there. For one week, we were to be models of propriety!

Jack brought them to the ranch. Sally was a lovely young nurse and her mother a loving little lady who had reared a large family by herself after her husband had died. She had made a living by sewing and any other type of work she could do at home while caring for her growing family. As soon as Jack was gone, Joe and I "pulled out all the stops," and played all the pranks we knew on Sally. She was a wonderful sport and her mother enjoyed every bit of our naughtiness. Of course, we also quoted all the orders Jack had given us. One of our cousins from Denver was spending the summer with us and he and Sally had a water fight on the front lawn, so Joe and I weren't the only ones out of control.

We never knew what report Sally and Mrs. Forster gave Jack when he took them home. Despite what he probably heard, Sally married Jack. She was obviously happy to become a part of the family.

The summer I came home after my first year of college, I was feeling quite superior to Joe, who after all was still in high school. We went to Salida together and all was fine until we walked to F Street. That was the main street at that time and was lined with parking meters. Joe began to play leapfrog over each meter as we went along. I was embarrassed and tried to separate myself from him, but to avail. He would make a jump, then run up beside me and put his arms around me. That's how we processed along the sidewalk of the main businesses of Salida—much to my horror.

Before I entered the convent, Joe wanted to take me for a treat to a ski course. We had skied at home but just on a trail behind the house with toe straps to hold our feet on the skis, and no poles. We went up near Leadville, Colorado, to ski a course where there had been an army training camp—Camp Hale.

Joe paid for our tickets, skis, boots and poles. The tow line had T bars. Every time I tried to sit on one, it hit me on the back of my knees and knocked me down. Finally, I decided to pump my way up the course instead of riding. My dumb decision lasted for about one hundred yards, when the altitude got to me and I nearly passed out. I skied very carefully back to the bottom, turned in my equipment and rested in the car while Joe enjoyed the course.

When I was in high school, I often begged my brother, Jerry to take me on one of his all-day rides when he went to check the fences and our cattle on the summer range. After an early breakfast, we set out. It was a beautiful day, and I was thrilled to be allowed to go along. Little did I know what happens to one's legs after nine or ten hours in the saddle when one has not ridden more than an hour or two at a time at a much slower gait. The last miles of riding were pure agony, but I knew that if I got off the horse to walk, I wouldn't be able to get back on again. We were moving along at an easy trot, so there was no way I could keep up even if I could walk. We were in territory totally unfamiliar to me and at the end I would have had to walk alone across the fields of the reformatory—not a wise thing for a teenage girl to do. I rode on, thinking that at any minute I might fall off the horse from sheer exhaustion. We made it home, but it was all I could do to unsaddle, water the horse, and turn her loose in the pasture. I never begged to go along to check fences and cattle again.

I graduated from Buena Vista High School and received a scholarship to Mount St. Scholastica in Atchison, Kansas. I attended college there for three semesters, then entered the convent which was on the same campus. There I was known as Sister Elizabeth.

Often I am asked why I got to keep my baptismal name but Leann and Kathleen could not keep theirs. In those early years, we never used our family name except on legal papers. That made it necessary for each of our names to be unique. That was quite a job when we were several hundred sisters. There was a Sister Elizabeth before me, but she had died, so I was permitted to have Sister Elizabeth. Later, when we began to use our family names regularly, we were given the choice to go back to our baptismal name if we wished. Many of the sisters went back to their baptismal names. Leann said she had been Leander more years than she had been Amelia. Also, she had signed many legal papers using Leander when she was an administrator in a public school. Her choice was to shorten and feminize Leander to Leann.

The Birth of Joe and a Short Sketch of His Life

The third boy, Joseph (Joe), was born August 20, 1934. It was special for us girls, who knew only older brothers, to have a baby brother. Joe was now the center of attention. As they grew, Joe and Beth, being closest in age, became "buddies," as were Kathleen and Mary Margaret. After graduating from high school, Joe spent a year in California in an aeronautical school, learning to build and repair airplane engines so he would have that skill if he were to be drafted. After finishing the training, he returned to live and work on the ranch. Even as a youth he was an avid hunter and an expert fly fisherman. In addition, he explored many areas in the local hills, streams, and mountains. This experience gave him valuable knowledge of accessible trails and the best ways in and out of areas. When he joined the Buena Vista Sheriff's Patrol Search and Rescue North Team, his familiarity with wilderness places was very useful to searchers. At times, via radio, he directed helicopter pilots to injured hikers who were in places not accessible on foot. He first worked as a volunteer with Search and Rescue because he could not afford the $1 per month fee they charged for membership. Soon they asked him to be a member with no monthly fee. Joe says this was because he was strong of back and weak of mind! He also belonged to the Northern Chaffee County Fire Fighters Association based at Nathrop, for many years.

When Mom died in March, 1956, Dad and Joe were left alone on the ranch. Joe was sole caregiver to Dad who was losing his sight from glaucoma and in a couple of years was totally blind. Until Joe was married, Georgie, a neighbor very close to us all, kept her promise made to our dying mother of periodically stopping on her way home to see if they needed anything and to visit with Dad. Georgie taught in Buena Vista and lived at Nathrop, so she passed the ranch each day of the week. She most often stopped on Friday evenings when she had more time to visit with Dad. Dad was very grateful and looked forward to Georgie's visits. Mary Margaret and Norman also came when they were able. That was difficult because Mary Margaret worked nights as a nurse while Norman was home with the kids; Norman was out farming in the daytime when Mary Margaret slept and took care of the kids. Joe enjoyed the long evening hours listening to Dad tell stories of the exciting early days when he had lived in train section houses at high altitudes. He also shared a lot of stories of the early days of homesteading and ranching. Dad had a wonderful memory and Joe learned about the early roundup days including many funny episodes. One story Dad told Joe took place on a ranch in South Park where the riders often stopped for a delicious dinner. One cowboy, relatively new to the group enjoyed his dinner and accepted a homemade cream puff for dessert. Taking a big bite, he got up from the table, ran outside and spit it out. When he came back in, he was visibly shaken saying, "That so and so biscuit was raw in the middle."

In later years, since Joe had learned so much early history from Dad about the area, the forest rangers asked him for many evenings to entertain and educate the summer tourists as well as local individuals about protecting the environment. He used slides from actual photographs the forest service had taken to show the heavily eroded land of earlier years. Then with photographs of the present land, taken from the exact same location, he showed the great environmental changes after ranchers and forest rangers had cooperated in developing and practicing safe and effective grazing practices. Joe, with his great sense of humor, also inserted many stories of early settlers in the area and Dad's old-time friends, which made an evening of wonderful entertainment. He also entertained local women's clubs with Dad's stories.

In 1960, Joe married Arlene Struna whom he had met when she was receptionist and secretary for Dad's lawyer in Salida. They had three children, a girl and two boys. The two who married live with their spouses in their own homes on the ranch and raised their children there.

When the new bride, Arlene, moved into the house she was very respectful and good to Dad. Although she brought her own furniture, she left the outlay of the house as it was. She put a chair where there had been a chair, the couch in the same place, and so on, so Dad could still get around the house safely and unassisted. Dad had diabetes so Arlene was very careful that he had proper food. Although Arlene prefers to take care of the kitchen and wash dishes, herself, she understood Dad's desire to be of help. So, with the help of the wire, pulley, and handle contraption that Joe had set up, Dad could go to the woodpile and bring in wood for the kitchen. Arlene washed the dishes and put them in the drainer. Dad stood beside her, dried the dishes and put them on the cabinet for Arlene to put away later. How many new brides would be that thoughtful?

At the time of Dad's death in 1961. the ranch had multiple owners. Dad and Uncle Bill owned it until Uncle Bill died after having been hit by a train. He did not have a will so Uncle Bill's portion of the ranch was further divided with Aunt Lizzie, Bill Jr., and Anne each with part ownership. Then Dad further divided the ranch in his will. Jerry and Vivian moved to Alaska, which left Joe to run the ranch alone. Accounting for multiple ownership besides running the ranch alone was a major task. It took years of saving money and much legal work to gradually purchase the portions owned by other members of the two families. The ranch, big enough to support one family, was finally under single ownership. However, there were two special pieces of land Dad had wanted to buy, both because of their usefulness and because of their pristine beauty. The first piece of land was surrounded by the national forest land where our family had grazing rights. By waiting and saving, Joe was finally able to obtain this area known locally as Tetersville. Then in 1981, 507 acres of native grassland in Chubb Park, including the headwaters of Trout Creek, came up for auction. Joe made the highest bid. After a few years, Joe had this new land titled as "Conservatory Easement Land." The 507 acres can never be used for development purposes of any kind; the land cannot be subdivided and only one home could be built on it. It can be used for limited grazing but it cannot it be used for exotic animals, because the fences needed for those animals would disturb the pattern of elk movement through the seasons of the year. To enjoy the beauty of this conservation easement, from the western side of Trout Creek Pass on Colorado Highway 24, look toward the north and east. The natural meadow with the foothills reaching to the Buffalo Peaks is a beautiful scene. (Dad called this a vega, a word from the Basque meaning a tract of land, according to Webster Unabridged.) Having worked closely with the forest rangers on conservation measures all the years we grazed cattle on the national forest, Dad would have supported this conservation easement one hundred percent. Our father's dream for the ranch was completed 50+ years after his death. For this accomplishment, Joe gives much credit to Arlene, saying that without her supporting him all the way, he could never have completed this task. At this present time, there are just a few homestead ranches in the entire county that belong to a member of the original family.

CHAPTER VI
Memories of Mom and Dad and Family Activities

We three Benedictine sisters grew up with our other sister, Mary Margaret and our three brothers, Jack, Jerry, and Joe, under the loving, guidance of Mom and Dad. It was truly a blessed home with unlimited access to hills, valleys, meadows, and streams. We had just two rules when we went exploring, hunting, or fishing—provided our work was done: be home for the next meal and tell someone at home where we were going. If no one was home we were to leave a note on the kitchen table, in case they needed to find us. We were only two and a half or three miles from the Colorado State Reformatory and when a prisoner escaped, our parents wanted us home. Parental and family love coupled with many varied activities kept us happy and busy.

The ranch was one mile from our nearest neighbor. Our experiences of complete solitude, of our cattle, calves, horses, birds, and wild animals; of our exploring; and of our carrying out assigned responsibilities, all helped us mature and have a great appreciation of our loving God's abundant gifts. We know that living in such an atmosphere created within each of us a deep connection with nature and a perspective to value honesty with ourselves, with others, and to care for our environment.

Our parents were very special individuals. They were our primary models of Christian living. Their differences were settled in private. They were honest and trustworthy and helped other ranchers with their ranch work as well as with their personal problems if such were entrusted to either Mom or Dad. They never talked uncharitably about anyone—nor did we in their presence. They knew or figured out how to do ordinary things in extraordinary ways. They loved their God, each other, their family, and everyone they knew. They were courageous and unselfish. These qualities do not happen by chance. They are acquired gifts resulting from practice and hard work. They made these personal gifts their own by helping others and by taking risks to do important things on the ranch. They lived their lives with their God in caring for their family even while wondering from where their next dollar would come. They were thrifty and depended on themselves for a living with few conveniences, without a telephone, refrigerator, or a freezer. This cozy homestead home is where we learned to be grateful, to care for each other, to socialize, and to be generous to all because of our parents' example. During the Second World War, Mom and Dad purchased our first, small car battery-operated radio to listen to the news about the South Pacific area where their eldest son, our brother Jack, was stationed in a variety of places as a Marine.

We had many hungry men coming through our area looking for work when we were young. No matter what time of the day any man would come, Mom, always being hospitable, prepared a meal for them to eat outside our kitchen door, besides giving each a lunch for their next meal. We were taught that these men were "fathers" to other children and needed to be treated courteously, and given a good substantial meal. Now, with homes equipped with gas and electric stoves and special microwaves, it is impossible to imagine how Mom could always prepare a good, hot meal with a wood burning stove.

We had our ranch cattle, chickens, and milk cows and planted a large garden to help with our food. Our older brothers also raised rabbits which we enjoyed. Dad and Mom were always willing to share the food we had with those in need and did so in such a way that their giving never hurt those receiving their help, never injured their self-esteem.

The first example I wish to share happened during the depression. A couple, Jim and Georgie House, came to the area from Kansas with an adopted niece. They had $15.00, a few belongings, and nothing else. They stopped at the ranch of a neighbor who told them to go to Jack Cogan and they would be helped. And they came. Mom and Dad found a way. There was an old house on our hay ranch. It had only a pump for water in the kitchen and an outhouse. They could live there for taking care of the place. Jim could look for a job and Georgie could take care of their child and cook for our hay gang in the summer during haying season. They were given food from our cellar, and their car was filled with gasoline from our tank. Jim got a job taking mail to St. Elmo, and eventually they got on their feet. The niece, Myrtle was close to Amelia's age. After Myrtle became a nurse and left home, Jim died suddenly and Georgie became one of our family. During the time of her heavy grief she lived with us. Then she returned to the hay ranch, continued to raise her own garden, and turkeys. She taught school in a country school very close by. Since we often went to Salida on Saturdays for Dr. visits or other business we always let Georgie know she could go along. When she had to make a trip to Salida, she often took one of us if we had to see a doctor or dentist. In those days, there were no medical appointments—you just went and waited your turn. When Mom was dying, Georgie promised that she would look in on Dad and Joe to see if she could help with anything. That promise gave Mom much peace.

Two other examples of Mom and Dad's Christlike care of the needy included two ladies. One elderly lady lived by the train tracks. The firemen on the train dropped coal for her to use in her home. Mom and Dad had us take eggs to her. One day Mom gave us a hen to give to the lady so she would have some good meat. Instead of killing and eating the hen, she made it her pet. The hen sat on a chair, ate with her at the kitchen table and gifted her with an egg every day.

Another lady, Mrs. Grant, also lived alone in Buena Vista. After her husband left her, our parents knew of her poverty. To help her, Dad and Mom asked her to prepare a noonday meal for us school age children. We provided all the food; that way she was also able to have food for herself, yet she was doing something important for all of us. This was wonderful for us because Mrs. Grant lived within walking distance of our school, and she was an excellent cook. This arrangement worked well until the school was moved to a location too far for the younger children to walk, but was resumed later when everyone was old enough to walk that far, eat, and get back to class on time. As Mrs. Grant aged, cooking for us became too hard for her. Then we either ate in the school cafeteria, when there was one, or we carried our lunches. However, each school day, after school we continued to help Mrs. Grant with her chickens, her garden, and other chores she had for us. One day she was not feeling well and said she felt as if she were dying. Her one request was for us to go home and ask Mom to come soon to baptize her, which Mom did. She died shortly after that. Her death was difficult for all of us, because she had been our "Mom" away from home.

Besides our own siblings, periodically some cousins came to live temporarily with us because of illness and/or death a parent. One family of cousins in Denver sent one of their older children to the ranch each year for the summer to be away from the teenage problems of a large city. Other relatives came to spend their summer vacations with us. With these extra children and other relatives, it became necessary for our parents to enlarge the kitchen.

Our kitchen, the largest room in the house, had multiple uses. It became our family's place to cook, eat, study, and to play cards or board games. We never had a telephone so we entertained each other in a variety of ways. Some evenings Mom and Dad played cards with our neighbors in the kitchen while we entertained ourselves in the small front room or outside when we had warm weather. Many guests chose to sit in the kitchen instead of the front room so they could visit with Mom while she cooked.

The piano was in the front room. Some evenings Mom played the piano and Dad played the fiddle while we stood around and sang all the songs we knew. Many evenings we played cards, checkers, and other games. Daytimes, we did a variety of chores, hiked, fished, and searched our land for flint and Indian arrowheads. We always found and remembered the location for our next December's Christmas tree. In addition to our own tree, we also located one to be cut for Mrs. Grant, one for Georgie, and one for Sister Leann—we shipped Leann's to her in a gunny sack, when she was in Salisbury, Missouri and in Antonito, Colorado. On the flat top of a hill near home, one summer we even built a city, composed of a post office, grocery store, "five & ten," and a drug store. These were constructed out of small pinion tree branches. Our nieces and nephews tell us the remains of our city, though now caved in, are still there.

During the winter, we skied down the hill behind our home, and in the summer, we swam in our muddy and very cold swimming pool. We all fished on the Arkansas River, the meadow ditches, our own creek, and two neighbors' small streams. Mom and Dad often took us in the back of our Model T truck for family picnics and fishing. Once each summer they also took us on a one-day trip to Cañon City to visit our grandparents and other relatives. In the early years, our Model-T truck was our only means of transportation. Later we had the Model A Ford car and a used International truck. When we didn't all fit in the car, we rode on the flat bed of the truck.

As we were growing into our teenage years, we attended many country dances in the school gymnasium at Buena Vista, and in two, one-room school houses—one close by at Nathrop and one at Pine Creek, which was about twenty miles north of the ranch. Dad or our brothers were our drivers. Dad was, without a doubt, the best dancer in the area. He danced with everyone and never missed a dance all evening. These dances with our neighbors and friends were times of social enrichment for us as the dances were attended by everyone regardless of age. Every dance began at 8:00, paused a short while at midnight for refreshments, and ended at 2:00 am. It made getting up at 6:00 or 6:30 difficult, but the fun was worth it.

Once a month, we had mass in Buena Vista on the fourth Sunday of the month, but never on Christmas, Easter, or other holy days. On that fourth Sunday, a priest would come by train forty miles from Leadville, Colorado, and stay in a hotel in Buena Vista for that night. He would celebrate his first Mass on Sunday at the state reformatory and then come to our church, St. Rose of Lima, in Buena Vista. Beginning at nine o'clock, we would have confessions, mass, and benediction. After mass, the priest taught catechism. Mom always played the organ, and everyone who could sing helped to make our music. When we were small, Mom and Dad gave each of us a dime for the collection basket at mass, making us proud to put "our money" in the basket when it was passed.

Later when Mary Margaret and I were in high school, Buena Vista became a part of the newly formed Diocese of Pueblo. The new bishop gave our parish a full-time pastor, Father Paulinus Hammer from Holy Cross Abbey in Cañon City. On Sundays, Father Paulinus said his first Mass at the state reformatory, and his second mass at Buena Vista. On the third Sunday of every month, his second mass was at Fairplay, leaving the church in Buena Vista without a Sunday Mass. Having a full-time pastor didn't last long—about two years as it was impossible for a congregation of nine families to support him. After that, a Benedictine priest who taught at the Holy Cross Abbey during the week came to Buena Vista for the weekend. That worked better, and the Sunday schedule remained the same.

Amelia, Mary Margaret, Beth, and I, together with Jerry and Joe, worked with our Dad, Uncle Bill, and Uncle Bill's son, Bill, Jr. in the hay field each summer. Dad and Uncle Bill had purchased another hay ranch south of Nathrop in 1929, making it necessary for us, when we were old enough, to help with the yearly harvest. At first Dad and all on the ranch, including Amelia, used horse-and/or mule-drawn mowers, rakes, bull rakes, and derricks. Later we used power vehicles instead of horses. Dad purchased a second-hand tractor to which he could attach a mower to cut the hay. Some old vehicles were retrofitted by our Dad and our brothers. These vehicles replaced horse-drawn equipment.

From mowing a field, Dad would approximate the size each stack would need to be for that year's yield. There was one permanent enclosure for two stacks on every forty acres of meadow. Within that enclosure, Dad would "step off" the perimeter for each stack and mark the four corners with forks of hay. Each load of hay was carefully stacked by hand, using pitch forks. The stack had to shed the rain and melting snow because if the hay got wet down in the stack, it would heat up and eventually catch fire. This stacking was a real art that took special skill. From setting the perimeter of the stack and approximating its height, Dad would know how many tons of hay a completed stack held.

When I was old enough to work, I drove the hoist, a car fitted with a drum in place of the drive shaft. This hoist rolled up the cable to raise a load of hay on the fork of the derrick to the top of the derrick and dump the hay onto the stack so the stackers could put it in place. In addition to running the hoist, I was responsible for keeping the area between the stack and the enclosing fence cleared. That was done by hand with a pitch fork. When Beth was old enough, she drove the hoist and I "graduated" to driving a bull rake which I used to gather up hay from the windrows onto the fork of the bull rake, drive it to the derrick and transfer the load of loose hay from the fork of the bull rake to the fork of the derrick, then go back to the field for another load. Jerry stacked hay, usually along with a hired man. Jerry was the boss around the stack. Mary Margaret drove a bull rake, and Joe used a side-delivery rake to put the cut hay, that had lain in the field long enough to dry, in windrows. He also drove a dump rake when windrows needed to be put into piles. We worked in the field for the entire month of August and some extra days in July and September. We enjoyed the hard work even though the work days were very long and extremely tiring. Each one of us was treated as an adult, and we all knew that we were contributing in a valuable way to our livelihood. During haying time, Dad would have needed to hire at least two or three men if we girls had not helped in the fields. Hiring more workers would have been financially impossible. Each one of us was thrilled to receive a silver dollar each year for our work.

Being alone in the fields was a blessing for us. It was a time and a place where we had space to individually enjoy the beauty of the mountains, hills, and our meadows. Often we saw various birds and even mice with little ones or a mother skunk leading her babies across the cut field. How we enjoyed the presence of our God who gifted us by showing us a large portion of His many treasures of nature!

After haying was finished and it was still warm, we girls worked with Dad and our brothers on our hillsides and creek bottoms to bring in our winter supply of dead pinion and cottonwood trees for cooking and heating our home. We enjoyed these days of real work besides having loads of fun with each other.

CHAPTER VII
The Loss of Our Parents

According to the convent's rules, during the time all three of us were members of Mount Saint Scholastica Convent in Atchison, Kansas, we were never allowed to return to our own homes except for the death of a parent. So, until we were missioned in Colorado, our chances to see Mom and Dad or any siblings were extremely limited. We did not have money for the trip by train and Atchison was too far to drive the Model T truck or later, the Model A Ford car. While Leann was still in formation, Mom's sister Emily and Emily's husband Chris Gelbach, made a trip by car to Kansas to see some relatives of Chris. They invited Mom and Dad to go with them. Mom and Dad had one or two days visit with Leann in Atchison that time. When Leann made final vows, Mom went alone by train to Atchison, to be there for the ceremony. What a joyful reunion! It would have been wonderful had Dad been there also, but at that time, he was busy with the hay harvest. When our brother Jerry and his bride Vivian were on their honeymoon, they drove first to Missouri to see Leann who was on mission teaching. That visit was very short but very important to the three of them. Also, Sister Leann had a short visit with me, when I was attending college in Atchison, and when she came there for several days before going to teach in Colorado. Finally, after nine years, when Leann was sent to Antonito, Colorado, she was close enough for Mom and Dad and family members still at home to be able to come to visit. Joe had been four years old and Beth six years old when Leann left home. At ages thirteen and fifteen they got to see her again.

In the summer of 1955, we three sisters were delighted to have both our mom and dad come from the ranch to visit us in Atchison. Mom and Dad enjoyed their visit, and Dad met and spent some time visiting with another sister's father, each sharing their knowledge about the actual building of many railroads in Colorado and Texas. After they left, I cautioned Leann and Elizabeth that we would be called home before many months because Mom's eyes were so yellow. The call came just five months later. Mom had exploratory surgery on February 13, 1956 at the hospital in Salida. She was found to be in the final stage of metastatic ovarian cancer which had spread to the abdominal and chest cavities and would very soon go to her brain. All the family came home because it was evident that she would not live long. The doctor had told Mom she needed to go to Denver for treatment. He also told the family about his plans for her. He added that we should not tell Mom how bad her diagnosis was. Our brother, Jack, spoke immediately and told the doctor that he would tell her the truth because she would want to know that her days were numbered. When he told Mom, with all of us present, she was not surprised at her diagnosis and said, "It's all right. I am ready. Just don't hang on to my apron strings. I know all of you will live good lives after I am gone." We three could only stay three days at that time but would be allowed to return when her death was imminent.

After about two weeks in the hospital, she developed blood clots in her lungs. Mary Margaret, our married sister worked as a night nurse there at the hospital where Mom was a patient. Mary Margaret bathed Mom each morning, and made sure she had the best of care. On March 12, Mom had her sixty-first birthday. By March 19, she had become comatose. Mary Margaret asked the doctor if we should be called. He said Mom might last up to a month. Mary Margaret listened to her own intuition and called the family members to come home saying she thought Mom would only last about 48 hours. The next day we all arrived. That was a very sad time to realize that Mom was in a dying condition and to see Dad in such deep grief. That night sister Leann and I remained with Mom through the night, holding her hand and praying for her. At about 6 a.m. the next morning,

March 21, 1956, the Feast of St. Benedict, Mom reached both hands to the corner of the ceiling in her room, called out and with a surprised and glowing smile dropped her arms and without any struggle, quietly died.

Mom had always played the organ at church. She had been special friends with a lady and her husband who lived across the street from the parish church. Mom once told them that when she got to heaven, she wanted to play a big pipe organ. Later, the morning of Mom's death, one of our family members called this couple to tell them about Mom's death. The lady said she already knew that Mom had died because at six o'clock that morning, both she and her husband had heard beautiful organ music. He went to check the church but no one was there and the music had stopped.

Her death was extremely difficult for Dad, who at that time was nearly blind. However, Joe our younger brother, took excellent care of him on the ranch. Joe connected a guy wire between the kitchen door jam and the wood pile giving Dad the freedom to go independently to the wood pile and back to the house without becoming lost. This also gave Dad a safe way to walk in the sunshine when Joe was at work in the meadows, or riding to care for the cattle.

For two weeks that first summer after Mom died, Leann, Elizabeth, and I were sent to Pueblo to teach vacation school. We were given special permission to go to the ranch on each of the three weekends to be with Dad. We traveled from Pueblo to Buena Vista by train. There a family member met us to take us to the ranch. Although Dad was still grieving, he and Joe enjoyed the long visits, and we got in some fishing too! Joe was taking wonderful care of Dad, doing all the household chores, cooking for him, and best of all, spending the long evening hours listening to Dad tell stories like the ones you have already read about.

When Joe and Arlene married, Dad's life was also enriched. Having a woman in the house whom Dad knew and Joe loved, was a great addition to their lives. Arlene was a lovely, gifted, unselfish, and wonderful wife and daughter-in-law. Because she gracefully accepted any help Dad could give, he was very proud to do something to help Arlene.

With Arlene on the ranch, things became more settled. Dad had some heart problems in the past, but always appeared to have his heart heal without any medical intervention. During one of these last times, he again had severe chest pains but refused to let Joe take him to the hospital. Instead he asked Joe to call their veterinarian to come "give me a shot like he gives the cows." Obviously, that did not happen. However, Joe called the family members home to see Dad. Again, the three sisters arrived from different missions. Dad rallied and began to feel better, so after several days, Sister Elizabeth and I returned to our teaching positions and Sister Leann to her administrative position. The evening before we left, Dad wanted to know how much our round-trip travel costs were. Although we said that was not necessary, he insisted. Sister Leann was figuring this out for him aloud, but he interrupted and said, "Just give me a total of all expenses, because the amount will be much less for me to pay than the cost of my funeral and burial."

On April 12, 1961, when Dad was finished drying the dishes, he felt tired and sat down to rest. He appeared to be all right, and Arlene told him that she was going outside to see Joe. She also told him to call should he need anything. A short time later when Joe and Arlene returned, they saw that Dad was pale and sweating profusely. He asked Joe to take him to the bathroom. Since he was cold, Arlene covered him with a blanket. Arlene called an ambulance, but by the time it arrived, Dad had died. He died without a struggle on April 12, 1961, at the age of eighty-three. After Dad's body had been removed they realized the "blanket" that had covered him was actually the hand-knitted bedspread Dad's mother had made and given to him and Mom for their wedding present!

CHAPTER VIII
Sister Leann's Education, Teaching, and Work Experiences

♣

Sister Leann has a B.S. degree in Biology from Mount St. Scholastica College in Atchison, Kansas, and attended summer school at the University of Iowa for Nuclear Biology with a National Science Foundation Grant. Teaching during the next school years, she attended classes in the summertime and received her Master's degree in Biology from Notre Dame University in Indiana.

Sister Leann—In Her Own Words

When I was a very young member in religious life, I took the lariat rope from my trunk, happily realizing I could show my classmates some of my ranch expertise. I coiled the rope, threw it, and easily caught one of my classmates in the dormitory. I did not know that my supervisor had seen my entire performance. Later, my supervisor laughed about it and told many sisters about my experience from my life on the ranch.

• • • • •

I taught for some years in St. Anthony grade school in Kansas City, Kansas. Besides teaching I was sacristan in the parish church. One day when I was dusting the high altar, I was standing on a high shelf of the altar dusting yet higher shelves. There I lost my balance, and beginning to fall, grabbed a large statue of the Blessed Mother causing it to tip. How well I remember that the statue was light in weight, but for some reason, it righted itself and neither the statue nor I fell. To this day I remember this incident, and believe it was a true miracle.

• • • • •

Another year, I was missioned to teach in the Catholic grade school in Salisbury, Missouri. On my train trip from Atchison to Salisbury I was to take care of a sister who was using crutches. The porter had been duly warned to help this sister when she would depart the train. When arriving at our destination, it was necessary for me to take the crutches and to leave the train first, so the infirm sister could use both hands on the railings. The porter, seeing me at the top step fully garbed in my Benedictine habit, holding the two crutches, rushed up to me and caught me in a tight "bear hug." Having the breath knocked out of me, I was unable to resist and the porter triumphantly set me, the wrong sister, down on the ground. Only then was I able to get my breath and to explain to the porter that the sister needing help was waiting for him at the top of the steps.

• • • • •

I taught in grade and high schools in Missouri, Kansas, Iowa, and Colorado. I taught at Donnelly College in Kansas City and Mount St. Scholastica College in Atchison, both in Kansas. I was then sent to Antonito, Colorado, to teach in the high school where later I was asked to become the principal of the high school. Still later, after receiving my Administrative Specialist Degree from the University of Colorado, I became the superintendent of the large poverty-ridden school district in the southern San Luis Valley. During my years as superintendent, I applied for and received a variety of government poverty grants for the school district. Other superintendents in the Valley came to me for advice when they applied for similar grants for their schools.

• • • • •

One semester Sister Kathleen and I were both in Antonito, Colorado. Knowing we liked to fish, the school maintenance man and an electrician, whom we knew, took us on a fishing trip. Wearing our long black garb, we were thrilled to go to a neighbor's pond which had been stocked with some rainbow trout. We went early in the morning and for a time the fish were not biting. To sneak a little rest, I placed my fishing rod in the back of the truck, and climbed into the truck cab to rest. All at once, I heard my rod traveling out of the truck. Jumping out to retrieve my fishing pole, I was surprised to see my fish hook imbedded in some fur next to a cow's horn. Trying to free herself, the cow kept backing away from me pulling more line from my fishing reel. Hoping to get some help, I looked to my fishing buddies, but they were rolling in the grass laughing and shrieking when they saw me pulling on my rod trying to free the cow. I had no choice but to break my line. To this day, I have clearly remembered the mighty pull of a one-thousand-pound beef hooked on my fish line. Truly that was the biggest "fish" I had ever caught.

• • • • •

In 1971, our sisters teaching school in Antonito were challenged by some individuals who came from outside the San Luis Valley because we "religious sisters" were teaching there in a public school. At the same time a man from elsewhere came to Antonito determined to replace me as superintendent. All of this caused many difficulties in town and the entire area. After some frightening circumstances involving safety issues, I was deputized and given a gun for my own protection. I never sat at my desk at night when I worked in my office because I feared for my life. With all of this happening, it became necessary for our sisters to resign at the end of the school year and permanently leave Antonito. How sad this was because our Benedictine sisters had staffed the grade and high school beginning in 1934 when the school district had no monies for education. Our Benedictine sisters came from Atchison, Kansas, and initially worked for no salaries for a time to open the school. The people in Antonito and surrounding ranchers had helped them by giving them food. Our sisters staffed many positions there until all resigned in 1971 at which time the school board had to contract new teachers to fill the vacated positions in grade and high school.

During the same year, 1971, all the Catholic schools in the diocese of Pueblo were closed leaving many of our sisters without teaching jobs and searching for other employment. So in 1971, I was back at Benet Hill, becoming one of our first members to "hit the streets" looking for a job. College teachers were plentiful at that time, so there were no job openings. After spending six weeks of writing resumes, taking tests, and having interviews, Joe Reich, a very good friend of our religious community, called to inform me that there was a Civil Service job opening for a nun at Fort Carson, just south of Colorado Springs. The day after my interview I was hired as the Catholic Director of Religious Education for the soldiers and their families.

Immediately, I was told to report for work there the next morning. The staff chaplain there was anxious for me to learn the ways of the army. In my years there, I especially enjoyed taking teenagers and military chaperons on weekend camping hikes in the mountains. Fort Carson buses would leave us off at the first trailhead, then pick us up one or two days later at the end of the trail. In my entire life, I was always looking to new possibilities, so while working my full-time job at Ft. Carson, I took classes in my off-duty time to become a Certified Hospital Chaplain.

Leaving Fort Carson, after eleven years there, I served as a Hospital Chaplain at Fitzsimmons Army Hospital in Aurora, Colorado, for two years while I lived with my Benedictine sisters in Aurora. In 1983, at age sixty-five, I became a hospital chaplain at Penrose Hospital in Colorado Springs, where I served cancer patients until my retirement in 1989 at the age of seventy.

• • • • •

Never wishing to be classified as "retired," I freely stated that I was being "retreaded," for each new job opening. I met and became a good friend with a Mercy nun, who worked in a hospital in Guyana, South America. Believe it or not, I had always hoped, during my lifetime, to work in the foreign missions. Luckily, Guyana was an English-speaking country, and my Mercy friend encouraged me to go to Guyana to teach. There in 1979, I became a volunteer for one year to teach science to the nursing students. During that year, I also helped in the unpacking and organizing of enormous amounts of hospital supplies arriving from the United States and Canada needed in the hospital there.

In Guyana, traveling by both motor and row boat, even on alligator rivers, I was delighted to be given chances go into the rainforests to meet the Amerindians, missionary priests, and sisters from a variety of religious communities, besides many lay volunteers. My friends arranged for me to see many beautiful sights, including one of the historic water falls in a deep jungle. When my visa expired, I returned to Benet Hill even though I would have happily remained in Guyana temporarily or for as long I would have been needed.

• • • • •

What a variety of jobs I assumed for short periods of time after my return to Benet Hill. For a time, I supervised our maintenance men for the Benet Hill plant, including the convent buildings and our Benet Hill Academy. I volunteered for night duty in our infirmary and later helped at our retreat center in Black Forest cooking and cleaning for those coming for a time of quiet retreats or just a time of rest. I worked as Director of Religious education at our Lady of the Pines Parish to replace Sister Evangeline the years she was at Guantanamo Bay and San Salvador. During the years of 1996 to 1998, I tutored evenings with a group of volunteers in our Sister Liguori's adult learning program, helping students receive their Grade Equivalency Degrees (GEDs). During the daytime, I often volunteered at Penrose Hospital in transport and substituted as teacher in some Catholic grade schools.

For exercise, I made sure to swim at least three times a week at public pools. To keep my mind active, I read many books, and played Scrabble, Hand and Foot, and Mexican Train with our sisters at home. Until we moved to Benet Pines, I spent many hours each weekday driving my religious sisters to medical and dental appointments. That challenge, I really enjoyed!

During the fifty-year jubilee of our Benet Hill Monastery, I was thrilled to celebrate my seventy-fifth anniversary of my Benedictine vows by renewing them during our Sunday mass with a chapel filled with our sisters and many guests. I was given a standing ovation when completing this. How grateful I was, and still am, for the many years of being able to serve my dear God.

As this is being written, I live in our Progressive Health Care Center here at our Monastery. I need a little help at times, but remain independent. I attend Holy Mass, Community Prayers and meals while traveling with my trusted walker. I continue to read many books, papers, and magazines to keep busy. My favorite television programs include the daily news programs and a variety of sporting events, including the football games of Notre Dame, the Denver Broncos, and many other teams. I also enjoy basketball, softball, and golf on TV as well as *Jeopardy* and *Wheel of Fortune*. Fly fishing has always been my great love.

• • • • •

On May 3, 2016, I was surprised to get a special invitation from Adams State College in Alamosa, Colorado. I had been chosen along with other individuals to receive an award for the many years of our lives we had dedicated to education. At the celebration, we each were given a small, individual replica of the larger ones which were to be placed in the Adams State University "Educators Hall of Fame."

Someone had nominated me citing the many challenges in the poorest school district in the state of Colorado. Students there were grateful for all they had learned from me about education and ways to relate to the Hispanic culture.

The Master of Ceremonies congratulated me, "as retired at 97 years young." He gave a brief summary of the many states in which I had taught in grade schools, high schools, and colleges, as well as being the high school principal in Antonito and later becoming the district superintendent. When I was called to the podium to receive my award, I thanked everyone, especially those in the district, who had helped and supported me. My closing remark was, "All of this has transformed me and tamed me some. It's been a great ride."

From Sister Leann's autobiography, this following quote is her final paragraph:

"I think more and more about the end of my life, as so many of my relatives, classmates and friends have died. I think of death as a change of state, but not as an end, I believe in what Jesus taught us that He will be waiting along with those I have loved in life, who have gone before me. I am the eldest of a family of over one hundred fifty relatives, including brothers, sisters, nieces and nephews, and their many children and grandchildren, to five generations. It has been such a joy to have Sisters Elizabeth and Kathleen among my beloved Sister Benedictines."

Sister Leann's Death

It is with sadness, but great hope that I write that our Sister Leann, age 97, was called to her eternal reward on August 27, 2016. She was a remarkable, gracious, and joy-filled member of our Benedictine family here at Benet Hill Monastery for fifty-one years and, previously, a member of Mount Saint Scholastica Convent in Atchison, Kansas, for her initial twenty-five years of vowed life. When her life was fading away, she had such a happy smile as she greeted each person who came to say goodbye. Among the many who came was one of the teenagers originally from Fort Carson, now a grown man, who had enjoyed the weekend camping hikes with others his age when Leann led them into the high mountains. She wanted them to experience the awe, the joy, the beauty of the mountains and the solitude to be found there that she still remembered from her own youth.

CHAPTER IX
Sister Kathleen's Education and Work Experiences

Sister Kathleen holds a B.S. degree in Biology from Mount St. Scholastica College in Atchison, Kansas, and a Master's degree in Biology from St, Mary's College in Winona, Minnesota, and a B.S.N. in Nursing from the University of Colorado in Boulder, Colorado. She trained as a hospital chaplain in St. John's Hospital in Oxnard, California, and became a Certified Hospital Chaplain.

Sister Kathleen—In Her Own Words

Early in my teaching career, I was sent to replace a sister in Walsenburg, Colorado, who was on sick leave. My superior informed me that I would be teaching Biology, Chemistry, and English. I felt comfortable in saying that I could teach those classes. However, she asked me to also teach a small Latin I class. I told her that I had never had any Latin. She looked at me in disbelief, so I continued, "When I entered the convent, I studied some of the psalms we prayed in Latin, but never got very far with that plan." One time our Novice Mistress asked me what "fiat, fiat" meant. Quickly I answered, "It means 'stand up, stand up' because every time we pray those words, we always stand up." She told me that it meant "amen, amen." Someone else was assigned to teach Latin.

My first full year of teaching was in Ottawa, Kansas, in a newly built Catholic school. It was a beautiful city, but some non-Catholics were initially not very friendly to us sisters, so it took a while before we felt accepted there. We four sisters lived in a large house two doors from the church rectory. We felt lucky because the priest's own sister always prepared a full noon meal for us on school days. That gave each of us more free time to prepare our classes than we usually had while living on a small mission. In Ottawa, each of us had two grades in our classrooms.

During the first month of school, we had a heavy rain and heavy flooding. Finally, one day the children had to be taken out of the school by boats to other locations where their parents could meet them, and if possible, take them home. The school basement was flooded, causing all the new kitchen equipment to rust before the water could be taken out. How sad that was because the small parish had worked so hard to have a wonderful school complete where the students would even have hot lunches.

We were out of school for two weeks before we could again have classes. The second week we sisters were going over to the church to pray. As we were leaving, I smelled smoke. I complained about it, but although the superior was not too happy about what she thought was a false alarm, she called the pastor. He had the fire department come to check the source of the smoke. When the firemen came, they found loosely wrapped electric wiring smoldering on the ceiling of our unfinished basement, a problem caused by steam from the flood. Our electricity was turned off for two days until electricians came and made everything safe for us. Our entire house felt damp. One night when one of the sisters was going into her bedroom, she opened her door, and the entire plaster ceiling of her room collapsed. She was very lucky that it had not fallen after she was in bed.

• • • • •

One Saturday I was cooking dinner. I certainly was not an expert cook but decided to make some beef stew. I put the raw meat in the kettle with the carrots and potatoes and began to heat the mixture. After it had boiled for a little while, the meat remained quite red, so I decided that perhaps I should take the pieces of meat out to fry them before putting them back in the vegetable mixture. I took one piece of meat to taste, but it was hot and I inhaled it. With it caught in my throat, I found I could not breathe and needed to go for help. I tried to go around our open staircase to the next room where one of our sisters was giving piano lessons, but found I could not go that far, because I became dizzy and weak. I could not call for help, so I sat down on the stairs steps. Evidently I became unconscious and fell, making some noise because the next thing I knew I was on the floor and the sister who had been teaching in the next room wanted to know what had happened. The piece of meat on the floor reminded me that I had choked and only then did I realize that my falling head first off the steps and hitting the floor had knocked the meat not only out of my throat but even out of my mouth. That sister sent her student home and finished preparing the meal for me. I know for sure that my guardian angel given to me by my loving God had saved my life. I was extremely grateful to be alive and able to say many prayers of thanksgiving for my special gift of life.

• • • • •

One day a lady from the parish gave us a small pumpkin. I had never made a pie, but said I would bake the pumpkin and get it ready for a pie if someone else would make the pie. One sister who had eleven brothers and sisters in her family agreed she would make the pie. When the evening meal came, she cut the small pie into four pieces. One sister coughed and stated that it tasted "terrible." None of us could take more than one small bite, because it was certainly not edible. We asked Sister what recipe she had used for the pie filling. Well, she said, she had made the pie just like she had seen her mother making pumpkin pie; using many spices in the amounts she had seen her mother use for three pumpkin pies for twelve people. We all laughed and ate some canned fruit for dessert.

A few years later while I was teaching at St. Mary's grade school in Walsenburg, Colorado, I was assigned with Sister Venard to do sacristy work in the parish church. One morning when the two of us went early to church, I noticed there were ladies standing outside in the cold wind, waiting for the front church door to be opened. Sister and I went in the church through the sacristy door. I started to go through the church to open the front door for those outside, but after I went past the communion rail, I noticed that the two curtains on the penitents' side of the confessional were missing. As I started over to see what was wrong, the priest came out of the sacristy, and I motioned for him to help me check the problem. He came and quickly pulled open the curtain in the center of the priest's portion of the confessional. I could not believe my eyes. There was a seemingly unresponsive man wrapped in the missing red curtains with his tongue hanging out of his mouth! I thought he was dead and became very frightened. To his dying day, the priest claimed that in running to the safety of the sacristy, I had jumped the communion rail in my long black skirts.

Father woke the man and found out that the he had been waiting for the priests in the rectory to go to bed the previous night which is when they would shut off the alarm. Then he would have stolen the monies from the vigil light stands. He had become cold and wrapped himself with the red curtains to get warm. He never had the chance to get the money because he fell asleep. After Father woke him, he sent him out the side door. Since Sister Venard and I had been so frightened, we giggled during the entire mass and were unable to settle down until breakfast when our superior asked us what had happened. Then everyone laughed with us.

$$\bullet \bullet \bullet \bullet \bullet$$

I believe one of the most difficult things happening to me concerned one of my fifth-grade boys. He and his younger brother came to St. Mary's School primarily to be hidden from their father who would not expect them to be in a Catholic school. The parents were divorced and although the mother had full custody of her two boys, the father had warned her that if he ever found them, he would kill them. A policeman had been assigned to drive them back and forth to school in a well-marked police car. The policeman always drove them very close to the back door on the inside of the fenced playground. We had to keep the boys locked in our classrooms while the other students went to recess or were free to go to their homes for lunch. The other teacher and I had to be sure no one was in the lavatory when the boys needed to go there.

After the school day ended, the same policeman met them at the same outside door. Within a few weeks, our principal was notified that the boys and their mother had moved elsewhere and we were most grateful.

One night after dark, one of the sisters asked me to accompany her to school. We were in the school building only long enough for her to pick up some books and papers. As we came down the steps from the first floor to the landing just inside the back door, we saw a man coming quickly up the steps toward us from the basement. He had nearly caught up with us, but we ran as fast as we could out the door and across a section of the playground toward the back door of our convent. He chased us beyond the swings and we started calling for help. That scared him and he quit chasing us. I do not know where he went after that because all we could do was to get to safety in the convent. Our superior called the police, but they could not locate the man. I don't think I ever went to school again after dark.

• • • • •

During my years of teaching at St Joseph's High school in Beatrice, Nebraska, one thing I distinctly remember was that Monsignor Mock, the pastor at the church, asked me if he could attend my Trigonometry classes because he had never had a chance to learn that portion of mathematics. I told him I would be happy to have him in my class. He was an excellent student and his class-mates and I enjoyed his presence in class. It was an unusual chance for me to teach an eighty-five-year old priest.

• • • • •

I always laugh when I remember how a younger sister and I chased a bunch of trouble makers at night. A group of teenage boys had made a habit of throwing mud on the outside windows of our home chapel. We two sisters decided we would catch these boys. We were expecting this problem to happen on a Saturday night and had planned well. Dressed in our full garb, we also put on our long black cloaks and waited and listened for the mud to hit the windows. We had guessed right and ran out the back door in time to see the boys come around our house and run into the alley. We were young and were certain we could catch them. After running a block and gaining on them, the last runner in the group stopped and shouted for us to stop. The person, who appeared to be very small, said immediately, "I have never seen such a 'beeg' thing in my life chasing me." Much to our dismay, we had nearly caught the new young priest in the parish who had seen the mud throwing and took chase before we did. We had not yet met him. He kept repeating over and over, "I have never seen such a 'beeg' thing in my life chasing me." He had to be referring to me since the other sister was much smaller than I. Believe it or not, later he shared with all the sisters that when he was young in Ireland, he had trained for the Olympics. He never let everyone forget this episode. Thankfully, there was never another speck of mud thrown on the convent windows.

• • • • •

The last year I was in Beatrice, the parish officials decided we sisters needed a larger, better equipped place to live. At that time a house a few doors from our convent was being sold and the parish purchased it. To begin remodeling it they built a new section on the back of the newly purchased house with eight bedrooms with very nice private facilities. After accomplishing that, monies were not available to finish remodeling the remainder of the building, so we slept in the new section, but needed to use our old house for everything else.

All went as planned, until one night as we were sleeping, I was awakened by screaming from downstairs in the unfinished portion of our new building. I ran down the stairs in my pajamas and bare feet to find who was so frightened. Her continued screaming directed me well. I turned on every light switch I could find as I traveled along through the empty rooms. When I finally turned on the kitchen light, here was one of our young sisters standing next to a tall statue with her arms wrapped around it. I put my arms around her to quiet her, but she continued to shake for a long time. I had never seen anyone so frightened. When she realized, she was safe, she started to cry. I asked her what she was doing there and she said she came into the kitchen to get a fresh, cold drink of water as the water in her room was warm. In the dark she had bumped into the statue. I finally took her to her bedroom and settled myself in my own bed at 2:30 a.m. The next morning, we found out that our pastor had moved statues from a mission church that was closing and had stored them in our unused kitchen.

• • • • •

For many years, we three sisters spent time in the early summer teaching catechism in various parishes for students who were unable to attend Catholic schools. However, the first summer after Mom died, our superior sent a group of sisters, including the three of us Cogan Sisters to teach catechism to several hundred students in West Pueblo, Colorado. During those two weeks, we taught in the mornings with the afternoons free to prepare our classes and to rest. We and the sisters teaching at the cathedral all lived in the convent at the cathedral in downtown Pueblo. One night when the sisters were together saying Compline for their night prayers, the prayer leader bowed toward the superior and asked for a blessing. The superior hesitated for a moment, and just at that time the bird in the cuckoo clock came out and cuckooed ten times for ten o'clock. Everyone laughed and laughed making it difficult to finish prayers. Shortly after prayers the telephone rang. It was one of the priests informing us that several of them had come over earlier to bring us an ice cream treat, but there was so much laughing inside, we hadn't heard the doorbell. The priests came back and we all enjoyed the ice cream.

During those two weeks of teaching, Sister Elizabeth and I taught sixty students in the front pews of the church. Another sister taught a large group in the choir loft and Sister Leann taught some of the older students in the "Cry Room," making the church extremely crowded. The church, an old barracks, was not air conditioned and it was extremely hot, especially for us sisters in our long woolen habits. The noise level was critically high, causing difficulties in hearing, concentrating, and speaking for both teachers and students.

During Mass one morning, a small boy leaned over the pew and pinched the ears of the boy in front of him. What a scream ensued! Every morning the first thing on the schedule was Mass. The first day the children were anything but prayerful. Later that morning, Father Sierra asked the sisters to say a Rosary out loud during the Mass to quiet the children and keep them from crawling between pews.

At the beginning of each day, the children had to walk great distances over weed-infested, dusty ground to come to the church. When they arrived, naturally they were thirsty. There was one hose with running water outside lying on the ground. Each youngster would drink from the hose and then drop it back on the ground for the next one to drink. There was only one bathroom inside available for all, but it proved sufficient for the morning hours. One day a child lost his shoe down a prairie dog hole. The child cried when Father Sierra could not reach the shoe even using a shovel. Father kindly took the little boy into town and purchased a new pair of shoes for him.

The Saturday before the First Communion Mass, Father Sierra told Sister Elizabeth and me that at times parents brought children to make their First Communions even though they had never attended classes. He asked both of us to stand at the church door as the children marched in before Mass to not permit any child who had not attended our classes to march in the ranks. That morning all the boys were dressed in their finest clothing and the girls were beautiful in their white dresses and veils. It was impossible for Sister Elizabeth and me to distinguish which children we had taught because they all looked so different than when we had previously seen them. Afterward we were certain that some children who never had come to catechism did make their First Communion that day.

· · · · ·

My teaching experiences were quite diverse. From 1951 to 1958, I taught grade school students in Kansas, Missouri, and Colorado. From 1956, after receiving my Master's degree in Biology from St. Mary College in Winona, Minnesota, I taught high school science and mathematics in Nebraska and Colorado. These years in the classroom included Saint Mary's High School in Walsenburg and finally in the public high school in Antonito until 1971.

During Christmas vacation of my last year in Antonito, the members of the school board there, asked me to become high school principal to finish out the school year. I shall never forget that vacation, because during that free time, I changed my name from Mary Lambert, back to my birth name of Kathleen, and I also exchanged my full Benedictine habit for a modern black suit, with an abbreviated veil which showed my hair. When I began my new job as principal, most students never recognized me as having been Mary Lambert, a teacher in that same high school just two weeks earlier. After completing the year as requested, I returned to Benet Hill in Colorado Springs where I spent the next two years teaching science in our Benet Hill Academy.

When I was forty-six years old, I asked to leave teaching to finish my nursing education at the Colorado Medical Center in Denver, Colorado. I left Benet Hill and spent two years earning a B.S. in Nursing at the University of Colorado. My hope was that I would be able to care for our elderly sisters.

After graduating and returning to Benet Hill, I was employed at Penrose Hospital. First and for the longest part of my employment there, I worked in Newborn Care, including Newborn Intensive Care. Later, I taught patients who needed special knowledge and skills for self-care before they returned to their homes. These included people with diabetes, patients with new colostomies, and those needing to learn other self-care procedures. When another nurse took over the education area, I was asked to work with a social worker to begin the discharge program to shorten hospital patient days. Later, I assisted a pain physician with injections and other medical procedures.

The time came when I was needed to care for our elderly and infirm sisters as an RN. I held that position with the help of an LPN, until the spring of 1979, during which time I worked part-time in the infirmary and also taught science classes in our academy.

Soon I realized I was becoming older and decided that I would like to be trained as a hospital chaplain. For one entire year, beginning May 1, 1979, and finishing in June of 1980, I trained for hospital chaplaincy at St. John's Hospital in Oxnard, California, receiving my certification. I then returned to Benet Hill and worked for a short time in an office job at Penrose Hospital during which time I searched for either a chaplaincy or nursing job.

With my new chaplaincy credentials, I was hired as a hospital chaplain at Mercy Hospital in Iowa City, Iowa. I spent two years in that position. I returned to Benet Hill because I had missed the sisters at Benet Hill greatly and yearned to again be closer to the mountains and good fishing.

While I watched for job openings close to Benet Hill, a chaplaincy job was advertised at St. Thomas More Hospital with an adjoining nursing home in Cañon City, Colorado. I applied and was hired as a full-time chaplain. I lived with Benedictine Sisters missioned there from Yankton, South Dakota. There I was only thirty-five miles from my home at Benet Hill. However, in the spring of 1997, I was asked to return to Benet Hill Monastery to assist in the finance office. That was a great change in my life and a difficult one because in the office I worked on a computer and with numbers rather than being involved with a variety of people in totally different settings.

CHAPTER X
Sister Elizabeth's Education and Work Experiences

Sister Elizabeth received a B.S. in Elementary Education at Mount St. Scholastica College, a M.A.T. degree in Mathematics from St. Mary's College in Winona, Minnesota, and attended a summer National Science Foundation Grant program in Nuclear Physics at the University of Minnesota in Minneapolis.

Sister Elizabeth—In Her Own Words

Three days after my August 15, 1953 profession of temporary vows, I was sent to St. John the Evangelist Parish in Kansas City, Kansas, to teach fifty-five students in the third and fourth grades. City life was a major adjustment for me. The first day on mission our superior asked another sister to walk with me to Strong Avenue to show me about the traffic lights, as our mail box was on the other side of the street. Sister pushed the walk button and we waited for the walk light. When we had the green light, a car was coming too fast to stop. I balked at trying to cross with that car coming, but Sister took me by my scapular and literally pulled me across the street—my first introduction to city life! In the convent there, I had a private room for the first time in my life. Nights were hard for a while because I had never slept where I could not hear another person move, breathe, or snore. What I did hear was the unfamiliar traffic noise along Strong Avenue and the Santa Fe train freight yards a few blocks away. I taught there for three years, each year moving up one grade with my students—an unusual assignment requested by the pastor because one of the students was an at-risk child.

August 15, 1956, I made final profession of vows. That year I was missioned to teach in Wathena, Kansas, in a small rural Catholic school. Two nuns and one lay woman taught eight grades. I was assigned to the first and second grades, with nineteen students. What a change! Sister Mary Paschal, who was a renowned primary teacher, was the principal and taught sixth, seventh, and eighth grade students. Since I had never taught in those grades before, each evening Sister Mary Paschal went over my next day's lesson plans with me, giving me suggestions and guidance. Then we taught with our doors open so she could hear what was going on in my room. Once a week, she taught my little ones for one period while I taught music to her students. This worked out surprisingly well. However, in January of that school year, Sister Kathleen, still known as Sister Mary Lambert, was moved from Walsenburg to Antonito, and I was sent to Walsenburg to take Kathleen's fifty-five seventh graders. More than once during the rest of that year I was asked by one or more students, "Where is Sister Mary Lambert? She was such a NICE SISTER!" From Walsenburg I went to Capulin, Colorado, to a public grade school.

• • • • •

When I had entered the convent, the sisters did not drive, so my license expired. I destroyed it and thought nothing about it until the year the decision was made that each mission should have a car and at least one sister be licensed to drive. In Capulin, I was assigned to drive because I had prior experience with a standard shift. When I was on my home visit with Mary Margaret and Norman in Salida, I had to get a learner's permit since I did not have my old license nor did I know its number. So, I went on mission with only a learner's permit.

After things settled in the school year, I went to the county seat in Conejos, twenty-five miles away, for my license. Sister Alcuin, an elderly nun went with me. When I went for my test, I was asked for identification, but I had only my learner's permit. They wanted my birth certificate, but it was in Atchison, Kansas with all my personal records. I had just registered my teaching certificate in another part of the courthouse and offered to go to get that information— not allowed! Finally, I said I had my college transcript, but it was back in Capulin. He said that would be illegal but he would accept it if I would get it. When he had the transcript in hand, we started to the car for the road test. The examiner told Sister Alcuin she could not go with us. She said that she would go to visit her friend, Connie at the post office. Then she added, "Be sure to give her a license, she has driven without one long enough." I nearly went through the floor. He looked at me and asked me if I had driven myself to Conejos. I just said, "What does one do when there is not another driver?" He smiled a little and said, "That was not a fair question. Come, let's go for a drive." I finally got my license!

· · · · ·

One year when I was teaching in Capulin, we had come to Colorado Springs during a potato picking vacation. On the trip home we decided to go over an old pass near Westcliffe instead of going over LaVeta Pass. There were two drivers at that time on the Capulin mission, but the other sister who drove was with her parents in a car following us. We went through Cañon City and up Highway 50 to Texas Creek, where we turned from the highway onto a narrow road which would take us toward Westcliff. It was afternoon and the sun was making it hard to see, although I was wearing dark glasses—not Polaroids. All the way up Texas Creek, I had followed a little blue car because against the sun I could not see clearly enough to pass. Finally, we turned south on an open road where I knew we could pass safely. I pulled out, glanced at the speedometer— right on 60—I looked up again to see only the chrome of a car coming straight at me. Dad had told us repeatedly never to hit a car head on even if a brick wall were the only other option. I swerved to the right, although the blue car was right beside me. What happened next, I cannot explain. I was driving an old second-hand Cadillac that had a passing gear under the gas pedal. Instead of hitting the brake, I floor boarded the gas and the extra power shot us through in front of the blue car, just missing both it and the oncoming car. My natural reaction would have been to hit the brake, which would have been disastrous. I know angels were riding with us that day! It was the Feast of the Archangels and we always prayed to Archangel Raphael for safety when we got into the car.

The sisters with me were both reading so they saw nothing until they felt the surge of power. By the time they looked up we were clear. I managed to drive about one hundred yards; then my legs went into spasm and I could no longer control them. When I stopped, the car following us also stopped. I went back and asked the other sister to drive. Her father was so kind and good to me. He told me to get in and relax—we were all safe.

Later the sisters in the second car said they knew there was no way we were going to avoid disaster because they had seen the oncoming car that I had not seen when I pulled out to pass. The chrome that I saw was like a bad dream. From what they could see there was not room between the other two cars for the big Cadillac. Sister Brigida, our mission superior, was in the front passenger seat with me. Since she had not seen what had happened, I told her when we got home that I had almost killed her. She just looked at me and said, "I trust you," and she never mentioned it again. I was so shaken I had to talk about it, so I called Sister Leann who was in Antonito. Her response was a question. "What color dark glasses were you wearing and what color was the other car?" My dark glasses were brown and the other car was tan. She said she had just missed hitting a car which she did not see when she was wearing brown dark glasses when she was in Kansas City. For many nights following this incident, I would wake myself hitting the board at the bottom of my bed as if I were hitting the brake! Although I continued to drive for many years, I never again enjoyed it. When after spinal surgeries, my legs no longer responded quickly with my brain, I chose to stop driving.

Perhaps the most frightening time in my life was when we closed our Benet Hill Academy in Colorado Springs. We had left the laboratories as they were for four years in case we would decide to reopen the academy. When the time had passed, Sister Virginia and I were given the job of clearing out both the biology and chemistry/physics labs, selling what we could and donating what was useable to other schools. I had taught physics, so I knew the combination physics/chemistry lab well, but I knew nothing about the biology lab. One day I discovered a can in the very back corner of a bottom shelf in the biology lab. When I took the can from the shelf, the odor of ether was very strong. I asked Sister Virginia to bring a cart as I did not want to carry the can in my hand—too close to my nose! I took the can on the cart to the chemistry lab, put it under the hood, turned on the exhaust fan and went to report that we had something dangerous in the lab and needed help.

The police came first, then the fire department. They just looked through the glass into the hood, but did not open it because the rusted top and the odor in the room made it very clear what we had. They didn't call the hazardous materials truck immediately because it was rush hour, and they wouldn't move anything dangerous until later in the evening. We locked the lab and were told to stay out that part of the building. About 6:00 p.m., the special truck came towing a big cauldron-like vessel. Traffic was stopped with police on guard. A man covered in something that looked like metal came in, put the ether can in a small container, took it down to the street, and placed it in the cauldron. Then the truck pulling the caldron with the ether drove away under police escort. The firefighter who remained at the school said they would take it away from the city, and shoot it to explode it safely. He told us that if we had done anything to jar the can or had attempted to open it, the explosion would have destroyed a section of the building and us as well. I asked him why it was so potent. He said the ether had crystallized and was more explosive than dynamite. My Guardian Angel got many "Thank yous!"

• • • • •

In addition to Walsenburg and Capulin, I also taught in grade school in the Antonito public school, Saint Cajetans in Denver, and Sacred Heart in Colorado Springs. After I got my Master's degree, I taught in high school in Walsenburg. My last years of teaching were at our Benet Hill Academy in Colorado Springs. In addition to teaching upper math and physics in the academy, I was also working part time in the finance office of Benet Hill Monastery. When the academy closed in 1982, I began to work full time in the office. That assignment lasted until 2013 when the results of a serious TIA made it impossible for me to continue office work of any type. Since then I am fully retired.

CHAPTER XI
Fishing Careers and Other Adventures

Originally, each summer, Leann, Elizabeth, and I took our vacations together. We usually stayed one week with Mary Margaret and her husband, Norman in Salida, Colorado. They often took us fishing with them to O'Haver Lake near timberline and the stream coming down to join Poncha Creek. Mary Margaret always caught the most fish on these days. The high-altitude lake and streams were especially beautiful with the blue sky, the puffy white clouds, and the clear running water. The stillness became an easy and delightful area to rest and enjoy a quiet time together and with our well known and loveable God who had created such wonderfully beautiful places in His world.

While in Salida, we also fished the Arkansas River on land that belonged to Norman and Mary Margaret and the Colorado State Fish Hatchery. We always had great fun fishing there in late May and early June because during these early spring and summer days, the river was high, and extremely muddy. Those days, the fish were closer to the banks in holes and slower running waters. Those of us with fishing licenses were permitted to catch twelve fish each day and have twenty-four fish in our possession. Some fish were used for family meals; others were cleaned and frozen in plastic bags of water to bring home to the monastery. With these fish, we would then wait for a Sunday which we three were assigned to cook the Sunday meal at the monastery. Then we fried and deboned the fish, preparing a delicious meal for the sisters and any guests who happened to be there that evening.

The other week of our vacations, we sisters lived with Joe and Arlene, often sleeping in the new home attached to Steve and Laurie's house. In later years, we also had a chance to visit with Brian, Steve and Laurie with their four children and Bruce and his wife Stacy with their three children. While on the home ranch, we fished on the Arkansas River, including along some land belonging to their neighbors. We also fished at Twin Lakes, Clear Creek Reservoir, and the lakes on Cottonwood Creek, all of which were north and west of Buena Vista. We sometimes fished on Trout Creek, especially after a rain storm because the water was a little murky then, so we didn't spook the fish. As we became older, Sister Elizabeth developed some health problems making her unable to go into the higher altitudes with Sister Leann and me. After that, she took her vacation time alone with Joe and Arlene as well as with Mary Margaret and Norman.

Elizabeth's Memories

One summer when I was visiting with Joe and Arlene at the ranch, there was a terrible storm and the creek in our yard flooded badly. After it was over, Joe went up the creek to the head gate to see how much damage had been done. I followed closely after Joe and when he saw me, he came through the mud holding something in his hand. He held out his hand to me and said, "Here, take this bird home and care for it." He was holding a baby hummingbird that had fallen out of its nest into the mud. The tiny bird was lying on its back in Joe's big calloused hand.

I said, "Joe, that bird is dead."

He answered, "No, it is not, I can feel its heart beat." Then its little legs began to move, so I went to the house with the bird not knowing how to care for it.

Arlene was home and gave me a bowl in which to put the tiny bird. The next question was how and what do you feed a baby hummingbird, which I began to call "Peanut." When Joe came in, he called the veterinarian to get answers. The vet said it was most important to get protein for the bird or it would not survive. We needed to find aphids, squash them and mix them with sugar water. We knew that aphids could be found on yucca plants certain times of the year. The season was too late at the ranch, so Joe and I went up Trout Creek to the east of home. Joe stopped and got out of the car several times looking for aphids, until he finally found some on the plants at the top of Trout Creek Pass. There we collected a good supply. Back home, Arlene gave us a syringe used for the calves. Without the needle, it was just right to offer Peanut his supper. Leary at first, he finally tasted it and approved, so the feeding question was temporarily solved.

When Peanut was strong enough, he would ride around on my index finger or as he preferred, on my thumb with my fingers sheltering him. Often I took him outside to teach him to drink from the bird feeder or the hollyhocks, but he would have nothing to do with either. He continued to be hand fed. He began to exercise his wings so I put a branch on the bowl for a perch, and he seemed to like sitting on it for exercise. One day he disappeared. Arlene and I looked over, around and in everything assuming he had fallen to the floor. No bird anywhere. That evening when I closed the drape on the window, there he sat behind the top edge of the drape looking down at me. He was hungry! I fed him and put a thin scarf over his home so he could not escape again.

One day when I had Peanut in the yard, a couple known by Joe from another state, stopped to visit Joe. They were amazed to see a humming bird riding on my finger. They were thrilled and took a picture of Peanut and me. I had hoped they would send Joe a picture, but they never did.

It was nearing time for me to leave and I didn't know what to do with Peanut. I thought maybe if I put him in the apple tree near the birdfeeder, he would go with the other hummingbirds drinking there or at least learn to use the birdfeeder or hollyhocks for his food. I left him there and went fishing.

When I returned, Arlene said to me, "Please will you get that bird out of the apple tree? He has done nothing but yell since you left him." Peanut came back into the house.

The day before I was to leave, I had him in the yard once more trying to get him to drink from the birdfeeder. Another hummingbird squealed and dive bombed us. Peanut took the challenge and flew away with the other bird. We never saw him again. Five or six summers later when I was home to visit, a hummingbird was found dead on the porch one morning. I still wonder if that was Peanut who had come home to die. I do not know their lifespan.

• • • • •

One summer on my home visit to the ranch, my niece Laurie invited me for a meal. The older kids were out in the yard where their dad Steve was working. The youngest boy, Kohl, about four years old, had chosen to stay and visit with me while Laurie was cooking. One of the older youngsters came in and asked his mother if they could play under the hose.

Laurie said "Yes, provided you will wear your swimming clothes and your dad stays with you."

My little friend disappeared and soon came to me in his swim shorts with the command. "Get on your swimming suit!"

I replied, "I don't have it with me."

Again, he insisted louder this time, "Put on your swimming suit!" I assured him my swimming suit was in Colorado Springs. He had the perfect solution for me: "Then just take off your clothes."

He went out to play while I continued to visit with Laurie. That night we had spaghetti, and I was trying hard to eat properly. Kohl was beside me watching me wrestle with my spaghetti.

Soon the announcement came, "Sister Elizabeth has a BIG MOUTH." Laurie laughed, but Steve looked horrified; although I was sure he was having a good silent laugh too. Very true is the saying, "Out of the mouth of babes." The last time I saw Kohl, he was taller than my six feet and I didn't even recognize him. How quickly time had gone.

• • • • •

I spent many summer vacations on the ranch with Arlene and Joe and in Salida with Norman and Mary Margaret. Each summer was different and very enjoyable. Some days they took me car riding. Out of many happy trips I will tell of two thrills for me.

Norman and Mary Margaret drove me over Monarch Pass and over Marshall Pass. Although I had lived within twenty miles of the foot of each pass, I had never been over either one. Joe and Arlene took me up on the hills to the northeast of Buena Vista to a high edge of a dirt road where I could see the whole valley far below. The view was great until he began to turn the car around on the narrow road—then I closed my eyes and prayed.

When I could no longer walk to the river in Salida, Norman or Mary Margaret would take me there in the car and give me their cell phone so I could call when I was finished and they would come for me. At the ranch, I was still able to walk to the river. Once, Joe took special care of me, when I could no longer stand for long at my favorite Arkansas River fishing hole. When I went to that hole the first day, there was a huge stump for me to sit on and for a backrest—a big goose feather standing proudly with the end stuck between the wood and the bark of the stump to be sure it was stable! Besides being grateful, I also had a good laugh.

Leann and Kathleen's Memories

One day, Sister Leann and I went up Chalk Creek to fish and stay in a friend's vacation cabin for two nights. What fun we had fishing at that elevation, 9,000 feet above sea level. We caught a few fish, but greatly enjoyed the forest there that was absolutely, fantastically beautiful. It was a place where one could stand quietly to thank our loving God for the beauty which appeared to us to be similar, we thought, to the beauty of heaven. That night we were very tired because of fishing up stream at that altitude, so we ate our packed lunch for supper and climbed into our beds. We were up early the next morning because of a noisy woodpecker working on a tree next to the cabin. We ate breakfast and again fished most of the day. That evening after we fried fresh trout and got out some other food we had, Sister Leann decided to take a shower. The only shower for the cabin was on the outside of the cabin.

Naturally the shower water was very cold since it was spring water out of the creek. Sister Leann thought it was truly wonderful, but I didn't even shower and was happy to go to bed immediately.

• • • • •

Perhaps the most dangerous thing that ever happened in our fishing careers happened one summer when we lived alone in our Sister Mary Margaret and Norman's home in Salida while they were vacationing out of state. We had fished one day on the Arkansas River which was at high flood stage. We caught some nice fish with worms along the banks. We ate our fish that night for supper. I complained to Sister Leann that I had lost many bait hooks because I did not get close to the bank because I was afraid I would fall into the roaring river. Sister Leann told me that she could reach down and get most of her hooks loose instead of breaking them off her line.

The next day we fished from a road next to the raging river. I was upstream from her and having a little luck. All at once I saw her farther down the road from me without her hat. I motioned for her to put on her hat because she so easily became badly sunburned. Instead of putting on her fishing hat she waved wildly for me to come to her. I hurried back to her as quickly as possible only to find her thoroughly covered with dripping, muddy water.

She told me that she had taken hold of a small tree and bent down to reach her fishhook to loosen it. Instead of supporting her, the little tree bent over and then straightened up, flipping her into the middle of the rapidly flowing river current. Our dad and brothers had taught us if we ever ended up in the river to always go with the current feet first so our heads would not hit the huge river rocks. She did just what she should have done. Since she had always been a strong swimmer, she got her breath, turned around, and swam against the current, returning to the exact spot where she had been thrown into the river. There her fishing pole was waiting for her with her hook still attached to the snag. She got hold of grasses and shrubs and got herself out of the river. Her hat and glasses were gone, but she was thrilled to be able to retrieve her undamaged fishing pole with its hook still attached to the snag on the side of the river. She and I had several problems. She was totally covered with mud, so after slowly walking up a steep hill to finally reach the car, I put my fishing jacket in the driver's seat for her to sit on so she wouldn't wreck the car upholstery.

We laughed a lot but were totally exhausted. We parked by the gate to the high fence around Mary Margaret's house, and I went through the house to let her into the back yard. There we took off her clothes and let her into the house where she could shower and dress in clean ones. Since we did not want to ruin our sister's wash machine, we took everything to the downtown laundromat. Their large washers and dryers took care of everything in good time. Since Sister Leann had a restriction to drive with her glasses, we still had to drive back the hundred miles to Colorado Springs to get her second pair. I often thought that had she drowned, we would have never known what had happened to her.

● ● ● ● ●

One of Sister Leann's and my greatest thrills of our lives took place when we went for a vacation to Fairbanks, Alaska, in July of 1978, to visit our brother Jerry, his wife Vivian, and some of their eleven growing and grown children who had remained in the Fairbanks area.

We left Colorado Springs and flew to Seattle, Washington, where we met our cousin, Sister Jeanne de Paul Esser, a Sister of Charity from the Cincinnati motherhouse. Sister Jeanne de Paul was a seventy-year-old retired nurse, Sister Leann was sixty, and I was fifty years old.

In Seattle, we stayed with our nephew Tom Cogan and his wife Jane. That night we enjoyed our visit with them. The next day they took us to Rainier National park but it was foggy and raining so we were unable to see Mount Rainier. On our way home, we stopped on a bridge high above the White River to get our first look at a white, murky river which comes from the melting of the glacier on Mount Rainier. Later we took a nature walk to the beautiful Grove of the Patriots. We had never seen such tall, huge, and beautiful trees. Jane prepared a delicious evening meal. Afterward we called our brother Jack, Tom's Dad, to wish him a happy birthday for the next day. We were tired so we retired early.

The next morning, Tom took us to the Boeing plant north of Seattle to see how the 747 airplanes were produced. Unreal! He told us that it takes six hundred pounds of paint to paint just one of those planes. Tom was so proud of Boeing and was looking forward to having the 747s coming out in 1983. We also came by the fish ladders where we saw the sockeye salmon jumping clear above the water.

When we got home, Tom and Jane started to cook our evening meal, but were interrupted by two phone calls from the ferry stating we had to be there at 4:00 p.m. We left our luscious chicken dinner behind and Tom took us to the ferry, only to find that we couldn't board until 5:30 p.m. and that our tickets were our boarding passes. We waited quite a distance from the water, waiting to move our heavy luggage to the ferry.

When we were to board, we knew we couldn't readily move our many pieces of luggage in one trip. Having traveled many times first class with her sister, Sister Jeanne de Paul kept asking for a red cap, but since none were available, Sister Leann asked me to stay with Sister Jeanne while Leann moved the heaviest pieces of our luggage on board. Sister Leann found spaces for us on the top floor in the ferry's solarium, and staked out our "pad." She then returned to help Jeanne and me carry the remainder of our belongings up under the plastic roofing which had many "Xs" marked on the roof above our places. What we didn't know was that each X marked where the roof leaked when it rained. On board the ferry, we were with many young couples with children as well as with many hippies.

The Ferry did not leave until 9:30 p.m. and we were hungry since, in our hurry, we had missed our dinner at Tom and Jane's house. We asked some lady to watch our belongings while we went downstairs to find something to eat. It was still day light at 11:00 p.m. so we could see some beautiful mountains and the rolling of the waves of the ocean. A little boy on my right side saw the label on my suitcase and was thrilled to know I was "a Real Sister." He was sleeping on a cot while we were fully clothed in sleeping bags on leaky air mattresses, which eventually left us on the floor. There the motor's vibrations made our spines suffer. Sister Leann did not sleep very well because when she stretched out, her feet kept hitting some man's head. I enjoyed everything, even waking up at 2:30 a.m. and finding it was still daylight. We got up at 7:00 a.m. when the other passengers were waking. There was a heat lamp on the ceiling of our solarium, which was hot but kept us dried out as the air was exceedingly moist and cool. We ate our breakfast consisting of breakfast bars and cocoa in our coveted "digs" under the Xs. We munched on candy bars which were old and dry because we had saved them for several months for this trip. Someone had told us that food on the ferry was expensive, so we had planned to save a little money.

I was happy that I had learned to sleep with my full purse in my sleeping bag, but my trust level improved as I saw everyone helping to keep other's things safe. We watched the ocean from the front of the ferry and played cards in the lunch area. Before we retired, we ate the cold fried chicken we had brought with us. We watched the hippies smoking pot and enjoying themselves in various ways. Everything became quiet at 9:00 p.m.

The next day it was foggy and raining. We ate our own breakfast in the lunch room and again played cards. We explored the rest of the ferry, even seeing where those with more adequate funds were staying. We bought and ate our supper rather early after which we stopped at Ketchikan, Wrangell, and Petersburg. We listened to a female park ranger's talk on whales and eagles. We saw whales playing around an iceberg, and saw two eagles in flight. It was raining heavily, so we moved our things from the solarium down to the dining room. We spent the night sleeping under the tables in the dining room where it was dusty, but warm and dry. During the night, we stopped at Juneau for about an hour for passengers to depart and others to board.

The next morning, we got up early to stuff our sleeping bags and organize all our belongings to be ready to depart at Skagway. When after having a very long stop at Haines, we finally left the ferry at Skagway only to discover that we had about a four block walk in an open field to get to the train depot from where we would travel to White Horse, Canada. A very nice man and his son carried our three heaviest suitcases or we may not have reached the train station on time. When we finally arrived at the station, we checked our luggage and got into one of the train's passenger cars. Each car had an old crock of chlorinated water for drinking. The strange thing was that the seats faced the middle aisle of the car. We finally decided that it was designed for the passengers to face each other rather than look down into the deep, deep river at the bottom far below us. Also across this deep chasm, we could see the wooden framework which held the train tracks we would soon traverse. We traveled through part of British Columbia to the Yukon.

To get to White Horse we went over a high, beautiful pass at timberline. I don't think I have ever seen such beauty, which looked like our loving God had prepared the scenery especially for us. On the other side of the pass, we stopped at Bennett, where we departed the train and were treated to a free meal in the cool outside air. The delicious meal of fresh bread, beef stew, beans, cheese, and apple pie was ready for us and for the people from a train going the other way. In all, about 300 people were given this special meal— such efficiency!

We arrived in White Horse at 5:30 p.m. and changed our money to Canadian currency. After checking in to a motel, we had to walk a long distance before finding a restaurant where we ate chopped steak sandwiches. Returning to the motel, we went to our beds, happy not to hear the loud motors we had suffered on the ferry. The silence and our beds were such a treat that we fell asleep instantly.

The next morning, we boarded a small Boeing 737 where each of us had window seats. We flew too high to see much scenery and crossed two time zones. We arrived at Fairbanks, Alaska, and went through customs. There we were met and taken home by our brother, Jerry and his wife Vivian, and some members of their family.

What a great time we had in Fairbanks. We visited the museum, went fishing, and had our first ride on a "paddle boat." One day we went toward the North Pole. We ate a picnic on the way. The mosquitoes were bigger and more numerous than I had ever seen. We went to the Yukon River near which a group of many men and women were "raising" a new home for some lady. I believe they accomplished that full job in one day.

One day in Fairbanks, Jerry said, "Today we are going fishing." We went to the grocery store, purchased many things, and the three of us sisters and Jerry left in his car traveling a long distance on a two-lane road heading to the place where a pilot Jerry knew lived. Since we would leave the next morning by plane to go fishing, we camped out that night amid many mosquitoes. We did not sleep very well because we were so excited. Early the next morning, we drove to the place where we met our bush pilot, who had an amphibious plane—a Grumman Widgeon. It looked like something we had seen only in pictures. We loaded up and took off from an extremely short runway.

As we climbed up into the blue sky, we saw below us, the forests which stretched for endless miles. We saw lakes and then more forests but not any sign of human beings or dwellings. Soon we saw a huge lake, one of the Tebay Lakes. In the distance at the edge of the lake was a huge, beautiful mountain of the Chugatch Range. We circled many times above the lake far below us to minimize the altitude to where we were going to land on the water. We were so excited that we could hardly wait to land on the water. We would remain all alone to fish beside that lake for three days when the plane would return for us. The beauty of the mountains mirrored in the lake was a little bit of heaven reminding us that our dear Lord had painted this exquisite place just for us.

The pilot had a small power boat in the plane in which he and Jerry placed our food and all our other supplies and fishing equipment. The two of them left, saying they would return in a short time. It was a long time before they returned. When they finally came back, Jerry got Sister Leann and me apart from Sister Jeanne to tell us that a large bear had torn one side off of the cabin where we were planning to live. Jerry and the pilot had put the cabin back together. He warned us to keep the knowledge of this frightening piece of evidence secret from Sister Jeanne.

We said goodbye to the pilot and were told he would return Tuesday to take us back to our car. Jerry put the three of us in the motor boat and took us up the side of the lake to the cabin. We arrived at our cabin without any trouble, unpacked the boat, and got the canned food and other supplies in the cabin.

Jerry wanted to take two of us fishing immediately. Because the motor boat could safely hold only three, I volunteered to stay on shore to fish that late afternoon. Those on the boat had a wonderful time but had caught no fish. On the other hand, I had caught eight beautiful twelve- to fourteen-inch rainbow trout. When the three returned, we rested and cooked our supper consisting of four of the fish, cold canned vegetables, and potato chips. Jerry put the other cleaned fish in a large, locked metal cooler box in the cold spring water next to the cabin, hoping no bears would come to try to get the fish.

We prepared for bed, using our sleeping bags. The mosquitoes were terrible! However, Jerry had brought mosquito repellent as well as sticky hanging objects to catch and kill them. Jerry warned us that since we were in bear country, if any one of us needed to go out during the night, he would accompany us with his gun to protect us. Believe it or not, we were grateful for that protection. However, we did not even see a bear the entire time we were there.

The next morning, Sister Leann was the one volunteering to remain on land while Jerry took Sister Jeanne and me out in the boat. Somehow, wading among many rocks in the cold water, Sister Leann broke her big toe and demolished her toe nail. Here we were with two nurses in our group, and not one of us had even an aspirin. Sister Leann, knowing her foot would swell, decided not to remove her boot. That night she was totally unable to sleep because of the pain, but suffered in silence so as not to disturb the rest of us. The next morning, she said she kept herself distracted during her sleepless night listening to the howling wolves.

I know we all caught fish that day, but I don't remember how many. However, we caught enough fish to fill our large cold box to take back to Jerry's home the next day. We all had much fun, except Sister Leann who was suffering with her painful big toe.

On Tuesday morning, we packed our things and got ready to wait for our "private plane. We cleaned the cabin and were careful to bag our trash to take with us. Once the pilot arrived, it did not take us long to pack everything in the plane. We flew out after moving the plane out far from the shore. We circled several times over the lake to gain enough altitude to get over the mountains. That circling over the lake gave us many angles from which we could see and remember all our lives God's natural beauty where we had been blessed to have spent the past days.

The trip back seemed to take much less time than our initial trip coming to the lake. We arrived at the very small private airport and thanked the wonderful pilot who safely had taken us to fish in such a beautiful spot with superb fishing. We loaded up Jerry's car and climbed in. It was a long trip back to Fairbanks where we first took Sister Leann to the emergency room at the hospital. A medic cared for her, removing the toenail and securing her big toe against the other toes. We were told that a medic, never a doctor, takes care of minor problems such as hers.

We were absolutely worn out but happy to reach Jerry and Vivian's home in Fairbanks. There Vivian had prepared a delicious, hot meal for us. We will never forget those wonderful days.

Our cousin, Sister Jeanne had been many places in the world traveling first class with her sister, but she said that during this trip, she had experienced more beauty than she had ever seen, and the trip was, by far, the best because she enjoyed so much fun.

· · · · ·

Another time Leann and I had a day of great fun was when she had just come back from Guyana, South America, and I had just come back from California. Not even thinking about the fact that we were not yet acclimated to the high Colorado altitude, we jumped at the chance when our brother Joe offered to take us to fish in the beaver dams near timberline on the east side of Buffalo Peaks, not far from our home ranch. He met us at a predetermined site on the highway near Hartsel, Colorado. We followed him up a narrow dirt road until we came to a fence, where we parked our car. Joe took us through a fence and we walked uphill toward the beaver dams to fish. Joe told us to continue that way by ourselves, because he had to go back to work on the ranch. He also added that he wanted us to call him at home that night before 10:00 p.m. to let him know that we were safely out of the high country. We reached the beautiful dams and had not fished very long when suddenly a thunder and lightning storm hit the area. In the mountains, lightning bounces from rock to rock and from hills to peaks, namely all over the place. We knew we needed to get to the safety of our car as quickly as possible. We folded our rods and took off. Each time we thought the lightning would hit again, we lowered ourselves to the ground. After the thunder, we got up and hurried before lying down again when it was time for the next lightning. We continued in this pattern until we were so breathless that we just had to stay on the ground to replenish our oxygen supply. We were not only exhausted but very thirsty, and we thought we would never get to the car. We finally reached the tree line, and slowed down a bit, but we still had a long way to go. At that altitude, we wondered if we would ever make it.

Finally, we reached the fence. Our first, happy thought was that we had drinking water in the car. We got to the car only to discover that the cows in that pasture had found something luscious on our car from the dried car wash. They had licked every inch of the car including all the windows. We had no choice but to wash the windows with our precious drinking water so we could safely drive the car. We drove back to Hartsel and used a phone in the filling station to call Joe to tell him we were safe. There we also bought each of us a can of pop.

• • • • •

Later that year, on a beautiful autumn day, we drove to the ranch to spend a Friday night because we wanted to leave early the next morning to go fishing. We went to a small stream originating high above the old, nearly deserted mining town of St. Elmo. We planned to go upstream to fish close to timberline. We parked our little Volkswagen Beatle a distance from the dirt road in an old rugged meadow. I was bait fishing ahead of Sister Lean as she was moving more slowly since she was fly fishing. I was having good luck, catching some pan-sized native trout. I came to a place in the creek bottom where I could not get through the brush. To get around the brush, I took hold of a tree limb and hoisted myself to higher ground. When I looked to see where I needed to go, there was a young man in a white T-shirt about twenty feet ahead of me. He had his gun pointed directly at me.

I yelled, "You fool," and dropped to the ground only to hear the bullet scream and hit the tree just where I had been standing. I was so frightened that I could hardly move. Thinking he might follow me. I slid down into the creek bottom and then ran some distance through the weeds, thistles, and low brush in the meadow. I was nearly breathless. I stopped and looking back, I could not see the man. Soon I saw Sister Leann down by the creek.

I shouted, "Sister Leann, come to the car now." She wanted to know why, but all I could do was to keep repeating myself as I headed for the car. She then came and opened the car door. I told her we needed to leave immediately. We collapsed our rods, she started the car, and we headed back to St. Elmo. We could not find anyone in the little town, and we did not have a cell phone, so we hurried back to Joe and Arlene's home on the ranch. After we calmed down, we decided that the young man was trying to frighten me out of the area because it was the day before deer season was to open, and he may have killed an illegal deer. It took me months to get my shins healed from my running through the overgrown meadow, even though I had worn a pair of jeans that day.

• • • • •

While I was in between jobs, our brother Jerry in Alaska called to tell us that he had a small Mazda car he had purchased for his grandson who had returned home to the Philippine Islands. The car was too small for other members of the family in Alaska. He was certain that we could use it at Benet Hill, but someone would have to come to get it. Sister Leann and I made a hurried offer to drive the car back to Colorado Springs. We kept very busy borrowing and gathering camping equipment to take with us on the plane. Sister Marie Therese spent several days helping us and getting one-way airline tickets for us to Fairbanks.

On July 4, 1996 after receiving the blessing for travelers from our sisters at Benet Hill, we flew to Fairbanks, Alaska. Four wonderful days of visiting followed. We saw the fine garden everyone in the family had planted and went to Jerry and Vivian's in-town home to see the huge, new garage and workshop Jerry had just finished building. His daughter-in law even had beehives there to have local honey to help her young daughter who had severe allergies. It was fun to be with Jerry, Vivian, and some of their younger children again. This time we also saw Christopher, their special needs son, whom we had not seen in twenty years. Chris was now living in Fairbanks. Two of Jerry and Vivian's sons left the next day to spear salmon on a river about 200 miles to the south of Fairbanks. To accomplish this, they tie themselves to trees and hang over the raging waters to get the salmon that pass directly below them. These fish will be frozen for food for the winter months.

Jerry bought a tire, a jack and a new wheel for the Mazda. He had the car checked carefully by the Mazda dealers. The two-door Mazda had been driven only 27,000 miles. What a superb gift for our community!

Finally, we said goodbye and headed for Colorado. After driving through many miles of road construction and heavy rain, we arrived in Tok, Alaska to visit Ruth Marie, one of Jerry and Vivian's married daughters, her husband Paul, and their four lovely children. We had a good visit and stayed overnight with them. We left early the next morning. We traveled slowly through much more road construction, and arrived at Haines Junction in Yukon.

We pitched our tents in a campground under a large tree. We were in our sleeping bags by 8 p.m. A heavy rain came during the night but inside the tent we remained dry, thanks to a good tent. We awoke at 4:30 a.m. to find that we were totally alone in the camp. We folded our tent and left in a heavy fog. Later in the morning we stopped by the road to stretch our legs and eat our Granola Bars for breakfast. However, I had a problem. I was tied fast to the car seat. I had dressed at the empty campground in the warmth of the car and had accidentally fastened my bra over the seat belt. To free me took some time. As soon as we started again, the fog was gone, and we had left the road construction behind us for a while.

Our next stop was the town of Watson Lake. Because the weather looked very threatening, we did not want to camp. The $87.00 price for a motel room prompted us to go to the Catholic hospital to ask if there were sisters living or working there. We found that the only sister who worked there was on vacation, but the lady taking care of that sister's dog invited us to her home for the night. What a gracious lady! She, Pauline Hickey, was a nurse from Great Britain who worked at the hospital. We were thrilled to have a dry, cozy room to sleep in that night. The next morning Pauline gave us eggs, hot ham sandwiches, and fruit for breakfast. What wonderful hospitality for us on the Feast of Saint Benedict! When we left, she gave us a huge box lunch, which lasted us through breakfast the next morning.

On the road again we drove past the cranberry bogs on the Liard River, a wonderful trout stream, and in the distance, a beautiful mountain peak. We saw several moose, one with a baby and a large, black bear. That evening, having crossed into British Columbia, we came to the Bucking Horse Hunter's Lodge out in the middle of nowhere. It was available for a reasonable price, and we were tired, so we stayed there for the night. The beds were clean, but the drinking water was a terrible brown color. We still had clean water with us so did not even brush our teeth in the dark water. Sister Leann said the water there reminded her of the water in Guyana.

The next day we made it to Dawson Creek where we ate pizza and camped on a lawn in a private campground. We got up early in a heavy fog, but could see a huge moon. Everything was soaking wet except our sleeping bags and mats, thanks to our big tent from Sister Marie Therese and the big plastic Jerry had given us for rainy nights. We left Dawson Creek in fog, but most road construction was finally behind us. By noon we were in Alberta. There we experienced the many miles of beautiful, large cultivated fields with blooming, yellow, canola plants. We had never seen canola before then. Our car looked like a mud hog so we went to a car wash using a hand spray to wash away the worst of the mud.

We drove through Edmonton and camped just outside of Banff Park. Here we found a refreshing cold swimming pool and a hot tub. We slept well outside in the first dry campsite of our trip. The next day, we drove through Banff and Jasper Parks. We also stopped a short time at Lake Louise. The mountains, glaciers, and lakes—everything we saw—was breathtaking! It felt as if a scene from Heaven was causing everything to be so unreal and exquisitely beautiful.

We made it to Calgary that evening and ate in a hospital dining room after not being able to find any fast food places. We called the Sisters of Charity of St. Louis de Montfort in Calgary. Yes, they had space and would love to have us stay that night with them. Four sisters lived there but two were on vacation, so we each had a full separate apartment for the night. They couldn't believe we had driven from Fairbanks and had camped several nights. They thought we had come for the Calgary Stampede which was being celebrated there, but Sister Leann told them that we were "stampeding" home to Colorado. That night we had a terrible rain, thunder, and lightning storm. Our dear Lord was always with us keeping us dry and safe.

On Saturday, we left Calgary after a wonderful visit and breakfast with the sisters. We traveled on a four-lane highway through beautiful farmland with the Rocky Mountains showing to the west. Toward evening we started looking for motels with reasonable prices, but every motel was full of visitors attending the rodeos. Every town of any size was having a rodeo. Finally, we found a motel room for two at Big Timber, Montana. From there we called Sister Elizabeth to report our presence in the U.S.

Sunday, we left early and found Mass in Billings, Montana, at The Holy Rosary Church. Sister Eileen, from the Leavenworth Kansas Charity Convent, was the parish administrator there. She gave a beautiful homily and played the organ. The young priest having Mass was deaf and dumb. He signed the entire Mass and a lady in the front pew read the complete text using a microphone. It was a beautiful Mass. Everyone had us tagged as sisters before we introduced ourselves. There was no resident priest there, so because it was a mission, a different priest came each Sunday to celebrate Mass.

In Montana, we drove through vast ranch lands. The ranch houses are hidden from the roads by the few trees which were left when the ranchers had cleared the land for hay fields. There was also much grazing land, but all the cattle must have been in the mountains for summer grazing as there were no cattle in any fields. Fishing streams were numerous and beautiful! We just drooled over them. Along the highway we saw many deer and antelope.

When we reached Casper, Wyoming, we called our cousin Marcia, and luckily found her at home. Marcia's brother Frank, and his wife Ellen were visiting their lawyer daughter in Cheyenne so we missed them. Marcia drove us up high onto the mesa above Casper to see the partly finished home Frank and Ellen were building in a beautiful grove of aspen and fir trees. It took us half an hour on a gravel road to return from their home site. We had a wonderful visit, supper, and night with Marcia. She is physically limited but is hired by the hospital to do special typing at home.